"Authority is the right t[...] nating in the Father, conferred upon us by Jesus through the Spirit. Chuck Pierce and Alemu Beeftu give us critical understanding of our authority and the times in *The King's Signet Ring*."

Rev. Dr. Kim Maas, founder, Kim Maas Ministries, Inc.;
author of *Prophetic Community* and
The Way of the Kingdom

"Inspirational and insightful, *The King's Signet Ring* encourages us to not only embrace our roar of revelation and treasures but to rush toward the awakening roar that will unlock heaven's changes into earth's atmosphere!"

Kent Mattox, senior pastor, Word Alive
International Outreach

"*The King's Signet Ring* presents a beautiful picture of the Kingdom authority God is releasing to His people to rule and reign in the earth. As you read, you will be empowered with divine favor to operate in your royal calling to become the signature of God to nations and generations."

Jane Hamon, senior leader, Vision Church @ Christian
International; author of *Dreams and Visions*
and *Declarations of Breakthrough*

"Chuck Pierce and Alemu Beeftu masterfully pen a powerful revelation that will unlock your identity in Christ and position you to access your Kingdom authority. The prophetic content written on these pages will reveal the mystery of *The King's Signet Ring* and how it symbolizes God's covenant with you. I highly recommend this book."

Joshua Giles, founder, Kingdom Embassy Worship Center
and Joshua Giles Ministries; author of *Prophetic Forecast*

THE King's SIGNET RING

UNDERSTANDING THE SIGNIFICANCE OF GOD'S COVENANT WITH YOU

CHUCK D. PIERCE
AND ALEMU BEEFTU

Chosen

a division of Baker Publishing Group
Minneapolis, Minnesota

© 2022 by Chuck D. Pierce and Alemu Beeftu

Published by Chosen Books
11400 Hampshire Avenue South
Minneapolis, Minnesota 55438
www.chosenbooks.com

Chosen Books is a division of
Baker Publishing Group, Grand Rapids, Michigan

Printed in the United States of America

All rights reserved. No part of this publication may be reproduced, stored in a retrieval system, or transmitted in any form or by any means—for example, electronic, photocopy, recording—without the prior written permission of the publisher. The only exception is brief quotations in printed reviews.

ISBN 978-0-8007-6255-1 (trade paper)
ISBN 978-1-4934-3746-7 (ebook)
ISBN 978-0-8007-6279-7 (casebound)
Library of Congress Cataloging-in-Publication Control Number: 2022008479

Unless otherwise indicated, Scripture quotations are from THE HOLY BIBLE, NEW INTERNATIONAL VERSION®, NIV® Copyright © 1973, 1978, 1984, 2011 by Biblica, Inc.® Used by permission. All rights reserved worldwide.

Scripture quotations labeled AMP are from the Amplified® Bible (AMP), copyright © 2015 by The Lockman Foundation. Used by permission. www.Lockman.org

Scripture quotations labeled BSB are from the Berean Bible (www.Berean.Bible), Berean Study Bible (BSB) © 2016–2020 by Bible Hub and Berean.Bible. Used by permission. All rights reserved.

Scripture quotations labeled CJB are from the Complete Jewish Bible by David H. Stern. Copyright © 1998. All rights reserved. Used by permission of Messianic Jewish Publishers, 6120 Day Long Lane, Clarksville, MD 21029. www.messianicjewish.net.

Scripture quotations labeled CSB have been taken from the Christian Standard Bible®, copyright © 2017 by Holman Bible Publishers. Used by permission. Christian Standard Bible® and CSB® are federally registered trademarks of Holman Bible Publishers.

Scripture quotations labeled ESV are from The Holy Bible, English Standard Version® (ESV®), copyright © 2001 by Crossway, a publishing ministry of Good News Publishers. Used by permission. All rights reserved. ESV Text Edition: 2016

Scripture quotations labeled ISV are from the International Standard Version. Copyright © 1995-2014 by ISV Foundation. ALL RIGHTS RESERVED INTERNATIONALLY. Used by permission of Davidson Press, LLC.

Scripture quotations labeled KJV are from the King James Version of the Bible.

Scripture quotations labeled NASB are from the (NASB®) New American Standard Bible®, Copyright © 1960, 1971, 1977, 1995, 2020 by The Lockman Foundation. Used by permission. All rights reserved. www.lockman.org

Scripture quotations labeled NET are from the NET Bible® copyright ©1996, 2019 by Biblical Studies Press, LLC Scripture quoted by permission. http://netbible.com. All rights reserved.

Scripture quotations labeled NIV1984 Scripture quotations are from THE HOLY BIBLE, NEW INTERNATIONAL VERSION®, NIV® Copyright © 1973, 1978, 1984, by Biblica, Inc.® Used by permission. All rights reserved worldwide.

Scripture quotations labeled NKJV are from the New King James Version®. Copyright © 1982 by Thomas Nelson. Used by permission. All rights reserved.

Scripture quotations labeled NLT are from the Holy Bible, New Living Translation, copyright © 1996, 2004, 2015 by Tyndale House Foundation. Used by permission of Tyndale House Publishers, Inc., Carol Stream, Illinois 60188. All rights reserved.

Scripture quotations labeled TPT are from The Passion Translation®. Copyright © 2017, 2018, 2020 by Passion & Fire Ministries, Inc. Used by permission. All rights reserved. ThePassionTranslation.com.

Identifying details of certain individuals have been obscured to protect their privacy.

Cover design by Rob Williams, InsideOut Creative Arts, Inc.

Baker Publishing Group publications use paper produced from sustainable forestry practices and post-consumer waste whenever possible.

22 23 24 25 26 27 28   7 6 5 4 3 2 1

CONTENTS

PART III · SIGNET RINGS IN THE NEW COVENANT

FOREWORD

I became keenly aware of wearing King Jesus' signet ring in 1976. I was in prayer regarding an upcoming mission to Guatemala when I heard the Lord say, *While you're there, I want you to be Me to the people.* I know that wasn't grammatically sound, but God was using this unique phraseology to get my attention. He had it! And the revelation of what He was communicating quickly followed: *You must represent Me. Be My hands, feet and voice; what You know I would do in a given situation, do it.* The concept of authority, of being "sent," of praying and speaking "in Christ's name," became much clearer that night.

The word *represent* means "to present again." A representative receives the plans and desires of another, then passes them on. Thus, they present again. The Lord was saying to me, "Present My heart and will to the people in Guatemala. Be Me to them." I went to Guatemala wearing His signet ring. Yet, if it's possible to be emboldened and intimidated at the same time, I was. I possessed new confidence, knowing I was sent by Christ and authorized to represent Him. But I wasn't so sure about "what you know I would do, do it."

Once in Guatemala, I traveled with a team to a remote village with no electrical power, plumbing or phones. This was truly in the middle of nowhere. We were on a humanitarian mission, building one-room huts for people displaced by the 1976 earthquake. At night, we would set up a generator in the middle of the village and preach the good news of Christ to them.

On the last night, I was asked to speak. Just before the service, I was told of a child who lived in the backyard of her parents' makeshift lean-to tied to a tree like a dog chained to a doghouse.

"She is insane," the parents had explained. "We can't control her. She hurts herself and others, and runs away if we turn her loose. There's nothing we can do, so we just keep her tied up." They were hours by car from any professional help, with no vehicles to take them there.

Just after I began speaking, the Holy Spirit said to me, *In your message, tell them you are going to pray for the little girl across the village tied to the tree in the name of the Savior you are preaching about. Tell them that through Christ's authority, you are going to break the evil powers controlling her, and that when she is normal, they will know what you are saying about Him is true.*

My heart skipped a beat. *I pray for headaches, not insanity*, I thought. As I stood considering this, the Lord spoke again, *Remember what I said to you before the trip: represent Me. This is not about your power or ability. It's about Mine. Do what you know I would do. Do it in My name—wear My ring!*

I told the people what I was about to do, then prayed. I pointed across the village and commanded the evil spirits to

let the girl go; I commanded her mind to function norı
She was set free, and the entire village came to Christ. ᵗᵘᵉ
King's signet ring sets captives free, mends broken hearts, heals
the sick and delivers from oppression! And heaven has a ring
sized to fit you!

Understanding authority is the key to spiritual success.
Jesus said He did nothing through His own authority while
on earth (John 5:30). He always and only represented His Father. Then He went a step further. Christ's understanding of
what it meant to move in the Father's delegated authority was
profound. He actually considered His actions to be those of
the Father who had sent and authorized Him. "It is the Father,
living in me, who is doing his work," Christ said (John 14:10).

Several years ago, I was preparing a teaching on the subject
of authority. If you have read any of my books, you know I
love to study words, weighing their origins, etymology and
different nuances of meaning. It was a given, therefore, that
I would look up the definitions of *authority* in my English
dictionary, then in my Hebrew and Greek lexicons. Better
than a day at the beach!

Some treasure hunters dig in the dirt, pan streams or dive in
deep water; still others peruse antique stores, flea markets or
garage sales. Hey, don't knock it—a New York family bought
a Chinese bowl for three dollars in a garage sale and sold it a
few years later for $2.23 million at Sotheby's. Different strokes,
as they say. The truly elite pursuer of hidden treasures, however, scours dictionaries!

As I lovingly searched in my original *Webster's Dictionary*,
which is heavy enough to use for a workout, I grew more and
more puzzled. I couldn't find the authority. My eyes traveled
up and down the page multiple times. How could I keep over-
looking this word? It had to be there. Finally, as I broadened

my search, it popped into my realm of vision as a derivative of the word *author*.

"Yes!" I screamed. "Word nugget!"

My wife could hear my excitement from the next room. "Are you reading the dictionary again?" she asked with concern in her voice. (She worries about me sometimes. Some people just don't get it.)

Authority flows from the concept of authorship. The person who creates something has authority over it, unless, of course, they sell it or give it away. The same is true with writing. Authors have authority over what they write. God has authority over all the earth because He created it. End of discussion, case closed. And He wants to share that authority with you.

The King wants you to wear His signet ring. He desperately needs and wants you to represent Him. There are certain principles and understandings you will need, however, in order for Him to fully do so. He has chosen to share them with you in this wonderful book, written by two giants of the Christian faith. I know of no two people who operate at higher levels of Kingdom authority than Chuck Pierce and Alemu Beeftu. As you read and embrace the truths in this book, you will find and wear the ring. And you, too, will hear Christ say, "Be Me to the people."

> Dutch Sheets, internationally recognized author, teacher and conference speaker and the author of *Intercessory Prayer*

INTRODUCTION

The Ring of Access

Chuck D. Pierce

One of my favorite trilogies is *The Lord of the Rings* by J. R. R. Tolkien. In the world that he created, all civilization rested upon the fate of one ring. A group of hobbits from the Shire set out on a journey to destroy the powerful ring. This ring that had been thought to be lost for centuries was found, and the main character, Frodo, embarks on an epic quest to destroy this ring.

In ancient times, rings were crafted and filled with power, signifying the ruling of others. In *The Lord of the Rings*, one ring had been created to rule the lesser rings of rule. This ring had the power to conquer all of the lands of the fantasy world called Middle Earth, and it would be used to bring all of the subjects into enslavement. The heroic journey of this troop depicts the power of a ring that is capable of ruling. The most obvious power of the ring was invisibility for the one who wears it. I know of no series of books that better reveals the true power of a ring.

Personally, I like rings. Anyone who knows me knows that I like a little "bling"! In *The King's Signet Ring*, however, we want you to understand the difference between decorative jewelry and wearing your authority. This book is about the power of the ring—*the signet*. A signet is the seal used officially to give personal authority to a document in lieu of a signature.

A signet ring was worn by a king or a high-level authority and extended the right for an individual to act on their behalf. The ring and seal of the ring are a symbol of covenant. A signet ring is a symbol of identity. A signet ring is a symbol of authority. A signet ring gives you access. The ring may be transferred from one generation to another. When two people enter into the covenant of marriage, most times they pledge their life by the exchange of a ring.

The ring may represent an era. Each pope still wears a signet, called the Fisherman's Ring, which is carved with a figure of Saint Peter encircled with the pope's name. After a pope's death, the ring is destroyed, and a new one is made for the next pope.[1]

You Are a Signet Ring!

I believe the Father actually intended His signet to go from one generation to another until His Son returns for the final ingathering of those who have followed Him through time.

Anne Tate, a key apostolic leader in the present-day watchman movement, shared this story:

> I lost my natural family through several crises. I lost my daughter. I had a son die at forty. And then my husband,

who worked for state agencies, died from a heart attack. I knew that I had influence and an anointing I needed to impart to another generation, but I had to watch carefully for the son and daughter that the Lord would align with me for the mantle I had been given by the Lord. The Lord brought Aaron and Tiffany Smith into my life as His restorative plan for my latter years.

During one of my trips to Israel, I purchased a ring with a gold coin encased in the setting. On Aaron's birthday I gave him a mantle, representing my spiritual authority, and the ring as a signet to carry forth my call and destiny in the future. I knew that the Smiths' three precious children would also receive this inheritance.

After the ring was given, Aaron came to me three days later to explain that he had lost the ring. We looked everywhere. He was devastated. I finally looked at him and said, "Son, it is not the object that is important but the spiritual significance of the impartation for your future that the Spirit of the Lord desires to rest upon you."[2]

You, too, are a signet ring. Dr. Alemu Beeftu will explain this more fully in the following chapters. God is seeking "seekers" from one generation to another generation. When these generational seekers align, the signet and mantle of the promise are extended. We find this in Genesis 22, when Abraham brought Isaac to Mount Moriah. Abraham was willing to give his only son (his entire future) to the Lord. The Lord intervened, however, and provided a sacrifice that was worthy to save Isaac and extend the future and lineage of Abraham. Once that happened, God then reiterated His covenant promise to Abraham but also extended it to Isaac.

You represent the King's authority on the earth. When we "put on" Yeshua, we are the Father's signet ring in the earth. Here are some Scriptures that I am praying for each of us (1 Corinthians 15:53; 2 Corinthians 1:22; Ephesians 6:11, 13 AMP). Let me write them as a declaration for you:

> For this perishable [part of us] must put on the imperishable [nature], and this mortal [part of us that is capable of dying] must put on immortality [which is freedom from death].

> He has also put His seal on us [that is, He has appropriated us and certified us as His] and has given us the [Holy] Spirit in our hearts as a pledge [like a security deposit to guarantee the fulfillment of His promise of eternal life].

> Put on the full armor of God [for His precepts are like the splendid armor of a heavily armed soldier], so that you may be able to [successfully] stand up against all the schemes *and* the strategies *and* the deceits of the devil . . . Therefore, put on the complete armor of God, so that you will be able to [successfully] resist *and* stand your ground in the evil day [of danger], and having done everything [that the crisis demands], to stand firm [in your place, fully prepared, immovable, victorious].

And I invite you to pray them out loud as a declaration over yourself.

Receive Your New Mantle and Ring

I serve as an apostolic leader of an international ministry. This ministry touches God's Kingdom people throughout the world. Approximately 180 nations sign in with us during the month to hear the Father's marching orders from heaven.

We are known as a prophetic portal that conveys the heart and mind of God to people around the globe. We also have a Spirit-filled service that is striving to be the Tabernacle of David restored in this generation. David's Tabernacle had singers, dancers, musicians and prophetic revelation on a daily basis. This was prophesied by the prophet Amos in chapter 9 of his book. This was reiterated by the early apostolic leaders of the Church in Acts 15.

We believe in God's order. He has first principles throughout the Word. First, His Spirit brooded to bring order to the earth. As civilization developed and covenant was established with Abraham and extended to his descendants, the tribes from each leading child developed. The twelve tribes eventually comprised the whole nation of Israel, His firstborn nation. The Lord then had an order for authority in war: Judah (praise), the fourth son's tribe, was to go first. Judah was the apostolic, prophetic troop who knew how to use sound to defeat the enemies in their inheritance. David was from this tribe. Yeshua was from this tribe. By the Spirit, the redemptive qualities of this tribe have been extended to each of us.

A Signet Assignment

Recently I gave an assignment to the Judah team in this ministry to develop two musicals representing the key times we are living in. I asked them to use the book of Esther for Purim and the book of Ruth for Pentecost. The musicals were amazing. The messages from each musical were more revelational and capturing than most that I have ever seen. Our recent production from Glory of Zion International at the Global Spheres Center on the life of Esther was called

Born for a Time Like This! Justin Rana, one of our Judah team leaders, wrote,

> One of the things that stood out to me in the preparation
> was the realization that in some way, we are all Esthers. In
> fact, some of the crew and staff kept having disagreements
> about how we were presenting Esther because you could
> not really tell which person Esther was in the production
> at times . . . but that was the point! Esther wasn't only a
> person in history, but a full-blown example of the char-
> acter of integrity for today, which she displayed, and how
> we should each demonstrate our call. The most incredible
> impacting aspect of her life was her dying to self and in
> turn receiving the favor of the King. I wanted to be like
> her each day in my own life.[3]

Esther is a wonderful book, representing the times we live in today. Esther is a book of hostility—and a book of divine connection. Esther is a book of preparation that leads to submission. Esther is a book of boldness that reveals many points that help each of us in developing our destiny today. Esther is a book of war that leads to possessing the gates of your enemy. The key to understanding the turn of events in this book has to do with Esther boldly entering into the "inner court" of the king, and gaining favor in the inner court before him. When asked by the king about her desire, she extended an invitation to the king to attend a celebra-tion and to bring the enemy of her people's future to this incredible feast. Once she left the inner court, she had no fear to confront her enemy.

As many of you know, in the story, her enemy was exposed at the celebration. Instead of the enemy's plan to destroy the Jews in Shushan, Haman was hung on his own gallows. This reveals to each of us the power of faith. But when Esther asked to overthrow the decree that Haman convinced the king to sign for the destruction of all the Jews in that region, the king said to her, "I cannot reverse what my signet ring has sealed and ordained" (see Esther 8:8). But he instructed her that she *could* rally the Jews and go to war against this signet authority and they would be able to overthrow what had been decreed. She was eventually able to take out all ten of the sons that Haman had placed in leadership in the province. She was given the house of her enemy, Haman, a hater of the covenant seed—a modern-day antichrist, the Beast of his time. *But notice she had to go to war to overturn the decree of her enemy in the earth.* That is the power of a signet. Someone who is wearing a greater call for justice from heaven must overturn that decree. This is important as we continue into the political strife of nations in the days ahead.

Who Is in Control?

Do you know that we constantly utter the phrase "God is in control"? Many times we say this as a mantra—but have we relinquished control as Esther did? "God is in control" should not be a theoretical statement. It should be a statement of action, of opening your hands and letting go of every situation so God *can* direct your steps. We cannot *hope* that God is in control. We must unequivocally decree to our atmosphere, "God, we relinquish control to You. We remove ourselves. Guide us by Your hand." Only then can the King give us His signet—His signature of authority to rule and reign in every circumstance.

Imagine trying to overturn a situation in the heavens with your own signature. What power or authority would that hold? If we, as humans, proceed with ourselves as the controlling entity of our lives, then our own signet is all we have access to. If we turn over control to God Himself, however, we have access to the ultimate authority and can rule and reign with Him.

In 2020 the United States, like the rest of the world, was hit by the COVID-19 pandemic. One article noted, "On top of the millions of lives that hang in the balance, Cambridge University puts at \$82 trillion across five years the cost to the global economy of the current pandemic."[4] We are seeing a manifestation of governmental involvement around the world designed to "limit the human and economic impact of the COVID-19 pandemic" in today's times.[5] I believe many people have relinquished control to the wrong authority. We are here to stand against everything on earth that is against the will of God, who rules from the throne room.

While we must respect and honor those in authority on earth, we should never view government as the ultimate signet authority. God, our Creator, has the ultimate signet ring. Who do we place our faith in during times of crisis? Have we declared that God almighty has ultimate control of our lives and only *He* can sign off on what happens to us? Regardless of what is happening in and around you, God must still rule and reign in your life so He can make the decree that will *favor* us into your next place. Be like Esther—let go!

Change and Wear Your New Identity

Ruth is one of my favorite books. There is not a book that better reveals restoration, redemption and the unlocking of our future. Ruth had made covenant with her mother-in-law, Naomi, and they returned to the land where Naomi had an inheritance, Bethlehem. Ruth was faithful in her covenant with Naomi. She worked daily to glean the fields. This caused her to be noticed by the richest man in the region, Boaz.

There came a time when Naomi said, "Ruth, we must make a shift. You must move from gleaning into favor for our harvest of the future" (paraphrased). Ruth was still wearing the widow's garment from when she lost her husband in Moab. In order to secure her future, the widowhood garment that was covering her had to come off. One of my favorite passages is Ruth 3:1–5 in the Amplified Bible:

> Then Naomi her mother-in-law said to Ruth, "My daughter, shall I not look for security and a home for you, so that it may be well with you? Now Boaz, with whose maids you were [working], is he not our relative? See now, he is winnowing barley at the threshing floor tonight. So wash and anoint yourself [with olive oil], then put on your [best] clothes, and go down to the threshing floor; but stay out of the man's sight until he has finished eating and drinking. When he lies down, notice the place where he is lying, and go and uncover his feet and lie down. Then he will tell you what to do." Ruth answered her, "I will do everything that you say."

Justin Rana also served as director for the musical production of Ruth. I have loved giving my signet ring to this next generation and watching what they can produce. One of my joys is when they begin to understand the lessons of

God through His characters that display faith. Justin said this about the book of Ruth and the musical:

> Another great example of relinquishing control to God is Ruth. In the recent Glory of Zion International production of *Threshed: A Shavuot Musical*, we portrayed the journey of Ruth and Naomi. This is one of the most significant stories in the Bible because without the absolute obedience and dying to self of Ruth and Naomi, the bloodline of Yeshua could not have been established in the timing God intended. I believe many times we just think, *Well, God is God, and He can do whatever He wants.* But we must remember, God gave us dominion over the earth. We must give up control to Him in order for His plans and purposes to be established fully. Therefore, had Ruth not stayed with Naomi and accompanied her to Bethlehem, she never would have come into contact with Boaz, and the bloodline would have been thwarted. The action of us letting go allows God to take the wheel. Even through what was probably a horrific experience for Ruth, being a foreigner, a Moabite, in the midst of a new land, she pressed on and made sure she did what needed to be done. Even more interesting is the fact that Ruth submitted to her authority (Naomi) when she was told to go lie at Boaz's feet. This seemed like it was a line Ruth was not willing to cross . . . she couldn't relinquish *that* much control . . . but she did it anyway! Ruth listened to a higher authority than herself, and ended up being part of establishing a bloodline that would affect the world until the end of time. Pause and think about that.

I wonder how many times we ignore the prompting of the Holy Spirit and instead take our own path on any given day. How many times do our brain and our logic override the Spirit within us? Suppose there was a prompting within a scientist that could have cured a disease, but they chose to ignore it because it didn't line up with their logic and they would have been ridiculed by their peers? Do you know that many people were prompted by an "internal feeling" (which we know as the Holy Spirit) not to board the flights on the morning of 9/11/2001? Many people actually listened and their lives continued on. So it was with Esther, Ruth, Naomi and several others in the Bible. We see a consistent theme of letting go and letting God. Let go![6]

When Ruth changed her garment, favor was fully extended to her. Then she entered into covenant with Boaz, and of course, the future of the Messiah coming to earth through man was unlocked. Your redemption was unlocked. The signet ring and favor go together. We wear this favor.

An Example of Wearing Favor

Joseph is another incredible example of faith in wearing favor and having a signet ring given to him. Joseph was given the double-portion inheritance from his father, Jacob. All the other sons knew that Joseph had been favored. His brothers removed this garment from him when they sold him into Egypt. Joseph gives an excellent example of walking in blessing. He went through many difficult times in his life. He was betrayed by his brothers, sold into slavery, falsely accused and thrown into prison. Blessing doesn't mean life is always easy. But Deuteronomy 28:7 promises that if you walk in God's blessing, your enemies

Blessing doesn't mean that you'll never have a battle, but God will enable you to win.

will come at you from one direction but flee before you in seven directions. Blessing doesn't mean that you will never have a battle, but God will enable you to win.

Joseph had some tough battles to fight. He faced many challenges that could have brought discouragement and defeat, but incredibly, wherever Joseph landed—he prospered. When Joseph was sold as a slave in Egypt,

> the LORD was with Joseph so that he prospered . . . When his master saw that the LORD was with him and that the LORD gave him success in everything he did, Joseph found favor in his eyes and became his attendant. Potiphar [his Egyptian master] put him in charge of his household, and he entrusted to his care everything he owned.
>
> Genesis 39:2–4, emphasis added

When Joseph was falsely accused and thrown into prison,

> the LORD was with him . . . So the warden put Joseph in charge of all those held in the prison, and he was made responsible for all that was done there. The warden paid no attention to anything under Joseph's care, because the LORD was with Joseph and gave him success in whatever he did.
>
> vv. 21–23

Like cream rising to the top, Joseph was able to rise to the top wherever he was. He eventually became one of the most powerful men in Egypt and was able to rescue his family from destruction. That's the power of blessing. God wants every believer to experience a blessed life. He wants you to rise to the top. He wants you always to be at the right place at the right time so you don't miss any windows of opportunity.

We wear the favor of God. . . . This is not a time for patching an old garment, but finding and wearing your new garment for your future (see Matthew 9).

This is a time to remove any old garment of death that represents your last season. Remember Lazarus. Jesus called him out of the tomb and removed all of his grave clothes (see John 11).

This is a time to receive new authority, as well as reconcile any relationships (both good and bad) that would keep you from moving into what is ahead. And then follow hard to develop your new identity. Remember Elijah and Elisha. That was another garment issue (see 1 Kings 19:19–21).

This is also a time to receive the outfit that represents your new position and assignment. Remember Joseph. He lost garment after garment, but finally ended up changing his clothes and ruling Egypt (see Genesis 41:13–14).

This is a time to remove and put on. Let the Lord dress you for the future. One of my favorite passages is Zechariah 3. The Lord reminded Satan that He knew all about the past of His people. But He said, "This is My time to reclothe them and move them forward."[7]

Divine appointments and supernatural connections are open doors to your future. That's the kind of life pictured in Jeremiah 29:11 and Romans 8:28. A blessed lifestyle is promised to every believer who meets God and walks humbly and obediently in His ways

You Have Unprecedented Access

Go boldly into His throne room. He is waiting. Be like Esther and ask for favor. Be like Joseph and wear a new mantle of favor wherever you are located. Favor, even in confinement, will open a new door of entry.

Ask the Lord to re-form the foundation for your standing. You may have to make a shift because the foundation you stood on in the past season is too shaky for you to stand on in the next season. Allow the Lord to solidify your stance so you walk in the fullness of what He will cause to blossom.

> Do not let *joy robbers* stop you from experiencing God's best. The Spirit of God will see to it that you celebrate. If you feel like your celebration is dwindling, just ask Him to release an anointing of *gladness*. This will sanctify you and cause you to press past that old season. Stop and hear the trees clap their hands.[8] When you hear the wind blowing in the mulberry trees,[9] you will receive a new strategy to come from behind and overtake the enemy that has blockaded your path. Watch where the winds blow. Catch the wind. You can catch up quickly. Move into that new place of victory. You will surprise the enemy. The Lord is saying, "I will give you cautions well in advance so you can shift the direction of your path."
>
> Ask for your root system to be reformed and that the roots of righteousness deep in you would be watered and begin to flourish. Ask the Lord to bring you past milk. Begin to digest the *protein* the Lord is giving you at this time. Declare that you will step through the gate of life into a new type of nourishment. Go out of your old place with joy, delight and happiness.
>
> Ask for a realignment of your heart desires with His heart desires. Then ask the Lord to allow you to hear the stillness of the heavens. In the midst of your chaos, ask Him to let you hear the stillness of His shadow. Ask Him to let you hear sounds you have not heard. Tell Him

you are listening and let Him circulate the atmosphere of heaven around you. Ask Him to bring and activate your atmospheric change. Let the cares of the day slip away so you hear the will of heaven. Don't go out in your own strength. Wait for the pulsating heart of God to propel forth the blood in your heart. Do not contend over how others are moving forward. Rid yourself of anxiety, and stop questioning how you will ever get everything done so you can advance into your best in days ahead.[10]

Ask the Lord what "one thing" you need to do to unlock your next phase. Jesus had to be baptized by John. Let your right standing come forth. The Lord is longing to crown you with righteousness. Don't allow the accuser's condemning voice to stop you from wearing that crown. Dominion comes when we wear the crown (see Psalm 9). We are the righteousness of God in Christ Jesus, but you must wear the crown of that righteousness. Our righteousness must become experiential. Stand in your righteousness. Set your face to obey and to do what will keep you in right standing so that the enemy can't accuse you later of not doing something you should have done.

Yeshua Came to Become Your Door of Access

As you read this book, I am asking the Lord to give you *access*. In the New Covenant dispensation, the enemy is blocked from entering the throne room. But you have access! The access will release power that will cause the enemy to flee. This is an era of firsts, new beginnings and Kingdom demonstration. First Corinthians 2:6–9 talks about God's secret plan and wisdom that did not originate from this present age, but before the ages, to bring us into glory. No matter how established you are, there will be new beginnings in your life, ministry and spheres of authority. We, the Body of Christ, must *manifest who we are and whom we represent.* The Lord is forming a new order in the earth realm from His Council Room.

This book will help you to

- gain access to a new move of the Spirit of God in your life.
- gain access to all the riches of your garden. That was the first premise of boundaries. Within our new boundaries are the manifestations of glory and the communion of our future.
- gain access to the Kingdom of God. We will understand the Kingdom of God within us and demonstrate Kingdom power within our sphere.
- gain access to the blessings of Abraham's covenant and align with Israel—God's First Nation.
- gain access to mysteries held in His Word. There must be a revival of the Word of God in the Body of Christ. (The Father gave Torah to Israel, and then the Son demonstrated His heart and mind to us.)
- gain access to a new timing, linked with harvest.
- gain access to the Ark and understand the procession of glory in our region.
- gain access to understanding the government of God in heaven and earth. This will mobilize an army for war.
- gain access to new sound that will produce movement. Judah goes first. We are poised to gain access to new songs that will break old cycles.

- gain access to the understanding of God's order in our land.

Part I of *The King's Signet Ring* will provide an overview of the history and significance of signet rings, different types of biblical covenants and other symbols of kingly authority besides the signet ring or seal: the kingly garment, crown, anointing, scepter and throne. The signet ring is a signature of secured or approved authority. Yet this authority depends upon the user's character. The proper use of the signet ring is for noble purposes by a king or his officials, as we have seen so far in the lives of Esther and Joseph.

We will examine more examples of how the seal of authority was used with the right motives in part II, "Signet Rings in Ancient Israel." The story of King Ahab and Jezebel is one notable example of a king's signature being used for evil purposes, however, by the king or his official—a complete misrepresentation of the signet ring. By contrast, the Bible mentions people who were treated as, and used as, signet rings of the Lord. One such person was Zerubbabel (see Haggai 2:23). Others were not specifically called signet rings of the Lord, but they were used by God in unique, powerful ways, like Zerubbabel.

In part III, we turn our attention to the signet ring in the New Covenant. First, we look at the link between the first man (Adam) and the second man (Jesus), then discuss Jesus as the signet ring of the Father and our High Priest. We will also highlight the sources of Jesus' authority: His Sonship, submission and service, the Spirit of God and sacrifice. The final chapter will unpack the Parable of the Prodigal Son in Luke 15. You will learn how the Father wants to bring you, His signet ring, back to your original relationship with Him.

He wants to restore your position and full authority in His Kingdom of glory.

———

Amber Pierce, my daughter-in-law, called me with a dream about access that is very significant. Amber lived through a traumatic childhood. As she says, however, the Lord was always there for her. She shares the full story about her family in the book that she and Daniel wrote last year, *Joy in the War*. The chapter "Moving through Trauma to Joy and Wholeness" captures the key points in her life. About her dream, she said,

> I was in a car with my mom and dad (both are now deceased). Daniel (my husband) and I were in the back seat, and my mom was driving. We were going through terrible traffic, across bridges and even through water. I was very concerned about my mother driving. My mother had multiple sclerosis and was very unstable while I was growing up. We ended up at my grandmother's house, where I stayed much of the time. Andrea Waitley, who discipled me, was at my grandmother's house. Chuck Pierce, my father-in-law, was there, and I also told him about my situation.
>
> When I turned to Andrea, I said, "I really don't want to ride anywhere in the future with my mother. I trust my dad or Daniel to drive." Andrea and I were sharing a room that I always slept in at my grandmother's home. This room had twin beds. I missed Daniel being there, but I knew the Lord had put Andrea in this setting with me. Andrea was put there to help me find the Lord. She represented a turn from my past to where I am today. When we went to turn down our beds to sleep, my bed

was full of valuable, valuable rings. They were very elaborate rings, all with precious jewels in them. I knew that many members of the church were present in this dream. I kept asking them, *"Have you lost any rings?"* Then I kept saying, *"These rings are available."*[11]

All dreams have some revelation in them. In this dream, you see the Lord revealing to Amber the tumultuous past she had to maneuver through. But the dream also shows there is stability and a place of refuge in the midst of your trials. Additionally, the dream reveals that the Lord has put people in our path to help us through our troubles. These people give us wisdom to disciple or teach us how to choose the more excellent way. Amber is now a very vibrant member and minister in the Body of Christ.

In the dream, all the rings in her bed reveal our future. Ephesians 2:6–8 in the Amplified Bible says,

> And He raised us up together with Him [when we believed], and seated us with Him in the heavenly places, [because we are] in Christ Jesus, [and He did this] so that in the ages to come He might [clearly] show the immeasurable and unsurpassed riches of His grace in [His] kindness toward us in Christ Jesus [by providing for our redemption]. For it is by grace [God's remarkable compassion and favor drawing you to Christ] that you have been saved [actually delivered from judgment and given eternal life] through faith. And this [salvation] is not of yourselves [not through your own effort], but it is the [undeserved, gracious] gift of God.

Reggie Crawford, a friend of ours, was also in her dream. Amber kept saying, "Reggie, come and get your ring!" Amber was actually extending a call to all of those in the Body of Christ to see what He has for them for the future. In Ephesians 3:8, 10 (AMP) we find

> this grace [which was undeserved] was graciously given, to proclaim to the Gentiles the good news of the incomprehensible riches of Christ [that spiritual wealth which no one can fully understand]. . . . So now through the church the multifaceted wisdom of God [in all its countless aspects] might now be made known [revealing the mystery] to the [angelic] rulers and authorities in the heavenly places.

His manifold wisdom is multifaceted and many colored. By putting on His manifold wisdom, we wear our signet ring and mantle into the future. This is like the coat that Joseph wore, signifying his inheritance. I want you each to know that you are to "wear" the signet that God has made you to be. No power or principality will be able to resist you. You are His workmanship. You are a handiwork and a masterpiece. He is the Author and Finisher of your faith. Wear your signet for the whole world to see.

As Amber said to Reggie, "Come and get your ring!" He is waiting on you.

PART I

SIGNET RINGS
Defined

1

The History and Significance of Signet Rings

Alemu Beeftu

Like clay is molded by a signet ring, the earth's hills and valleys then stand out like the colors of a garment.

Job 38:14 isv

Signet rings have been used for centuries. A signet ring is a timeless piece of history and is considered an heirloom. One journalist wrote, "The millennia-old symbols of family and personal identity are experiencing a popular resurgence. But how should you wear yours?"[1] That question, the tagline of a Bloomberg.com article, took me on a journey to discover the importance and relevance of signet rings in the Kingdom of God. In my studies, I quickly learned that before we can hope to answer the how of wearing a signet ring, we must first establish a common understanding of what a signet ring is and the lessons it holds for us today.

Often considered a gentleman's ring, signet rings have been used throughout history as a symbol of family heritage. Typically, a signet ring is designed with a family crest or another symbol representing an individual or family and is worn on the pinkie finger.[2] In the ancient world, signet rings, also known as *seals* or *signets*, were used universally. Authentic ancient documents contained a seal. Engraving was a common occupation in ancient days, and one of the greatest parts of the jewelry trade was to design custom-made signet rings with special symbols and emblems, created from gold and set with precious stones. Thus, seals and signet rings have been important throughout history.

In some ancient kingdoms, a king who wanted to mark or secure a document with his seal used his signet ring. He pressed it into softened wax and allowed it to harden into an unbroken seal that had the ring's mark. The signet ring represented the king's honor, authority and personal guarantee, which was something highly valued. In the Old Testament, these rings were used as a personal signature or as an emblem of authority. They were a portable instrument used like a signature today, but much more important. They were an emblem of authority that could seal or stamp a document, the door of a house or a tomb. Authentic ancient documents contained a seal. Engraving was a common occupation in ancient days, and one of the greatest parts of the trade was a custom-designed and finely crafted signet ring.

Signet rings are uncommon today and rarely used for their originally intended purpose as a seal. Today signet rings are worn in some spiritual organizations by bishops, priests and other clergy. Perhaps you have even seen them in your diocese, church or denomination.

What Do Signet Rings Signify?

Signet rings, historically, were worn for a variety of reasons and purposes. Some of these reasons include signifying beauty, wealth, identity, authority, seal or signature, promise (engagement ring), covenant (wedding ring), power, victory (championship ring) and affiliation (class ring). The basis for the recent popularity of signet rings is the combination of fashion and the prestige that the signet ring symbolizes.

Let's take a deeper look into the symbolism of signet rings.

Signet Rings as a Sign of Beauty

Because of their value, women of rank were adorned with rings and necklaces of gold. Since the time of Jacob, Israelite women wore gold rings on their fingers, ears or noses. Abraham's servant gave a nose ring to Rebekah (see Genesis 24:47). This practice became part of the Jewish culture and a sign of pride. "Zion's women are so haughty, and walk with outstretched necks, flirting with their eyes, prancing along as they walk, and making tinkling noises with their ankle bracelets . . . signet rings, nose rings" (Isaiah 3:16, 21 ISV). In those days, such rings were worn on hands, arms, ears and noses. The rings signified that women had a special beauty and grace. The Lord promised to beautify Israel as His Bride by lavishing upon her jewels: "I delight greatly in the LORD; my soul rejoices in my God. For he has clothed me with garments of salvation and arrayed me in a robe of his righteousness, as a bridegroom adorns his head like a priest, and as a bride adorns herself with her jewels" (Isaiah 61:10).

Signet Rings as a Sign of Wealth

By wearing signet rings, rich men distinguished themselves from others and showed their social position as wealthy individuals. We see rings such as these referenced throughout the Bible. In ancient Israel, gold rings were presented to the Lord as special gift offerings: "So we have brought as an offering to the LORD what each man obtained—articles of gold, armlets, bracelets, signet rings, earrings, necklaces—to make atonement for ourselves before the LORD" (Numbers 31:50).[3] When the Israelites brought offerings of a quantity of signet rings with other gold articles to Moses and the high priest Eleazar, they were accepted as special gifts to the Lord. We also see many instances where wealthy individuals made signet rings for their sons. In Luke's Parable of the Prodigal Son, the father, a man of considerable means, bestowed a ring upon the lost son who returned home (see chapter 8). Later in the New Testament, James challenged believers for showing favoritism because of gold rings and fine clothes among believers (see James 2:2).

Signet Rings as a Sign of Identity

In modern cultures, everybody carries some kind of identification: a driver's license, passport or another type of picture ID. Thousands of years ago, however, personalized identification took the form of a ring. In the Old Testament, this was illustrated for the first time when Judah propositioned his daughter-in-law, Tamar, who was disguised as a prostitute: "What pledge do you want me to give you?" he asked, to which she replied, "Your signet ring, cord, and the staff in your hand" (Genesis 38:18 ISV). Three months later, when Tamar discovered she was pregnant, "she sent this message to her father-in-law: 'I am pregnant by the man to whom these things belong. Furthermore,' she added, 'tell me to whom this signet ring, cord, and staff belongs'" (v. 25 ISV). When Judah saw the signet ring, he knew he had done wrong. The matter was settled because the signet ring proved his identity. There was no mistaking the identity it represented (see chapter 4 for more on the story of Judah and Tamar).

When Judah saw the signet ring, he knew he had done wrong. The matter was settled because the signet ring proved his identity.

Signet Rings as a Sign of Authentication

Kings had signet rings throughout history as a personal signature or seal. Signet rings were used to a great extent for sealing decrees or important documents as security, so they would not be opened, and they showed ownership by kings and officials (see Esther 3:12; 8:8, 10). Furthermore, signet rings sealed a written letter or official document as proof of the owner's original signature, or the document's originator. As such, signet rings are a form of a seal to show

- the source, authenticity and accuracy of the document
- the dependability of the message
- the authority of the sender
- the security of letter or document
- protection for the original message.

Usually, a ring engraved with some device is used for just such a purpose.

These types of signet rings used as seals are mentioned throughout the Old Testament as well as in ancient history (see Ezra, Nehemiah, Esther, 1 Kings and many other places in Scripture). In addition, according to *Easton's Bible Dictionary*, historic evidence, as well as archaeological remains, of such practices are found in many places. Here is one example:

> The use of a signet-ring by the monarch has recently received a remarkable illustration by the discovery of an impression of such a signet on fine clay at Koyunjik, the site of the ancient Nineveh. This seal appears to have been impressed from the bezel of a metallic finger-ring. It is an oval, 2 inches in length by 1 inch wide, and bears the image, name, and titles of the Egyptian king, Sabaco.[4]

Easton continued, "The actual signet rings of two Egyptian kings, Cheops and Horus, have been discovered."[5]

Any letter, document, decree or item deemed important enough would be sent out with the official stamp by the king's signet ring. That is what gave authority to the written official documents or decrees. Without it, they would just be paper. But since the king's signet ring was worn only by the king or his trusted official, everyone in the kingdom knew that anything with a seal of the signet ring on it was important and authentic. Whenever the king's subjects received documents that carried the seal of the king's signet ring, they were expected to obey, without question or delay.

Signet Rings of Ministry Commitment

Signet rings were used as a sign of commitment to a person or to the Lord, in addition to a variety of things. Personally, I wear rings for both reasons. I wear one on my left ring finger as a physical sign of the commitment I have made to my wife for the rest of my life. I also started wearing another ring on my right ring finger as a reminder of my commitment to the Lord's will and service.

In August 1978, when I left Ethiopia for further study abroad, Fellowship Church, my home church, gave me a ring with a bee on it. The bee symbolizes community, brightness and personal power. The bee is about discovering your new destination. The day I received that ring, I made a public vow to wear a ring on my right ring finger as a constant reminder of my call. Rings with Christian emblems are common and often worn among many denominations. Some church officials wear rings as a sign of their commitment to the church they serve.

Signet Rings as a Sign of Faith

Signet rings are a display of a covenant to certain belief systems. As believers in the Bible, covenants made with our heavenly Father in the Bible are first and foremost in our lives. By accepting Jesus Christ as his or her Savior and Lord who was crucified on the cross, each believer becomes a symbolic signet ring who carries His image and His glory.

That is what the Lord has been doing for His Church, as

> *By accepting Jesus Christ as his or her Savior and Lord who was crucified on the cross, each believer becomes a symbolic signet ring who carries His image and His glory.*

well. Because of His amazing and eternal love, He has been beautifying her for the final wedding of the Lamb (see Revelation 19:6–10). The apostle Paul wrote: "Christ loved the church and gave himself up for her to make her holy, cleansing her by the washing with water through the word, and to present her to himself as a radiant church, without stain or wrinkle or any other blemish, but holy and blameless" (Ephesians 5:25–27).

Why Are Signet Rings Relevant for Current Times?

The world, in general, is in disarray, from top global leaders to the grassroots people making decisions on a local level. Disorder continues into families, extended families and churches. Covenants are broken, overlooked, not implemented or canceled, causing a host of problems.

We, as believers in Jesus Christ, must look for solutions to reestablish order in our world. In studying Scripture, we see that biblical covenants were established to bring people together. The concept is not only a nice idea but a proven ideology that actually works when put into practice. A covenant represents ideas and a manner of thinking characteristic of a group, social class or individual. These same methods also work in businesses. We have forgotten the basics of establishing a strong covenant. A biblical covenant is how God has chosen to communicate, redeem and guarantee eternal life through Jesus. These truths, revealed in the Bible, are the basis of Christianity. The Bible is a covenant document.

My challenge for you is to read about the power of covenants—start to implement them. In the next chapter, we will take a closer look at the topic of covenants.

——— SIGNET RING DECREES ———

In Jesus' name, I decree that

- *I accept You, Jesus, as my Lord and Savior.*
- *I now receive the ring You have waiting for me.*
- *I am Your signet ring.*
- *I carry Your image and Your glory.*
- *I'm beautiful and priceless in Your sight.*

2

Signet Rings: The Seal for Commitment and Covenant

ALEMU BEEFTU

"'For this reason a man will leave his father and mother and be united to his wife, and the two will become one flesh'? So they are no longer two, but one flesh. Therefore what God has joined together, let no one separate."

Matthew 19:5–6

After I graduated from Grace Bible Institute in Jima, Ethiopia, I started working with a church that focused on reaching university students in Addis Ababa, Ethiopia. After five years full-time with Fellowship Church, I received a scholarship for further study overseas.

At my farewell, the church gave me a very special gift. That gift was a distinctive ring with a bee emblem. They presented it to me along with a charge that I should remember my covenant with the Lord to serve His people by bringing the best and sweetest to the spiritual with a diligent spirit. I accepted the challenge with great honor and the fear of the Lord. To this day, I wear two rings: one on my left finger as my lasting covenant with my bride, Genet Y. Beeftu, and one on my right ring finger, as a sign of my commitment and covenant to the Lord. I serve Him by feeding His people with the best I can offer. As a symbol of my commitment, I wear a ring with a lion emblem to declare the Lordship of the Lion of Judah.

From the beginning, God, our heavenly Father, has had covenants with humankind. Signet rings represent covenants. Historically, signet rings are a symbol of covenant. All authority begins with a covenant. This chapter explores the symbols of authority for God's purposes in the Kingdom of God.

Types of Covenants in the Bible

Looking into the biblical covenants, we are better equipped to achieve God's best in our spiritual lives and success in our daily lives. Oftentimes, we read Scriptures in the Bible but don't fully understand the covenants of God. Covenants bring authority when we operate in the right conditions. Several covenants are recorded in the Bible. I recommend that you not only read about the covenants but also study to receive their benefits.

Edenic Covenant

In the Garden of Eden, God gave humankind the mandate to procreate. The Edenic Covenant applies to all humanity.

He declared humankind has dominion over the earth and animals. There is no condition on this covenant. When God mandated this covenant, He promised to keep His promise and not change it. No requirements are required by humankind. "God blessed them and said to them, 'Be fruitful and increase in number; fill the earth and subdue it. Rule over the fish in the sea and the birds in the sky and over every living creature that moves on the ground'" (Genesis 1:28).

Noahic Covenant

In Genesis 9, the Noahic Covenant applies to all humanity and all other living creatures. When God saw the corruption and violence on earth, He sent the Great Flood to destroy all of humankind on earth except for Noah's family: four men and four women. All living creatures also were destroyed except for a male and female of each species. After the waters covered the earth, God declared that He would never send a great flood to earth again. He created a rainbow as a sign of the everlasting covenant between God and every living creature of all flesh that is on earth. The Great Flood was a reversal and renewal of creation. At that point, humankind and all living creatures would be fruitful and multiply, but it started again only through those that He selected.

Abrahamic Covenant

When God declared His covenant with Abraham, it was conditional—based upon his obedience to God. In Genesis, God instituted the first conditional covenant to Abraham when He said, "I will make your descendants as numerous as the stars in the sky and will give them all these lands, and through your offspring all nations on earth will be blessed, because Abraham obeyed me and did everything I required of him, keeping my commands, my decrees and my instructions" (26:4–5).

Mosaic Covenant

The Mosaic Covenant is found in Exodus, chapters 19 through 24, and the book of Deuteronomy. This covenant gave the foundations of the written Torah and oral Torah. God promises to make the Israelites His treasured possession among all people, a kingdom of priests and a holy nation, if they follow God's commandments. Part of the terms was given to Moses in the Ten Commandments. The Ten Commandments begins with Yahweh's identification and what He had done for Israel when they were brought out of the land of Egypt. He commanded absolute loyalty.

> "I am the LORD your God, who brought you out of Egypt, out of the land of slavery. You shall have no other gods before me. . . . for I, the LORD your God, am a jealous God, punishing the children for the sin of the parents to the third and fourth generation of those who hate me, but showing love to a thousand generations of those who love me and keep my commandments."
>
> Exodus 20:2–3, 5–6

Davidic Covenant

The Davidic Covenant originated during the reigns of Saul, David and Solomon. This covenant is unconditional and an important component in Jewish Messianism and Christian theology. In Jewish eschatology, the Messiah is believed to be the future Jewish king from the Davidic line. This king will be anointed with holy anointing oil and gather the Jews to return to the land of Israel. He will establish an era of peace and build the Third Temple, have a male heir, restore the Sanhedrin and rule as king over the Jewish people during the Messianic Age. This king will redeem all Jewish people and humanity.

The New Covenant

Jesus, in His perfect atoning sacrifice, delivered us from the curse of sin. The New Covenant, therefore, is a bond in blood sovereignly administered by God. The twisted thorn is a symbol of humankind's sin. The crown of thorns was intended to be a mockery, but it became a powerful symbol of Jesus and His purpose on earth. We, as children of the Most High, are continually reminded of the death, burial and resurrection of Jesus. Indeed, we are His inheritance.

Rings as a Sign of Covenant or Vow

Wedding rings originated with the common practice of betrothal rings used by the Romans, and later they were adopted by Christians. In modern culture, the betrothal ring is referred to as a promise ring or an engagement ring. The wedding ring is the final commitment of a lasting covenant between two people. The commitment starts with an engagement ring or promise ring. The promise ring simply says, "If you accept my proposal of a lasting covenant relationship, at the appointed time I will marry you or enter into a lasting covenant." Hence, a promise ring is given as a deposit. This practice is part of biblical history.

The seal of lasting covenant in the Old Testament was circumcision. The external sign of circumcision was a symbol of relationship that carried commitment in the form of a promise. It was like the engagement ring for Old Testament saints. God, the Giver of the promise, is faithful. That is what is so special to those who receive the promise, of circumcision. After Abraham received circumcision, a sign of covenant, he became a friend of God; even so, it was only a promise. The Lord used circumcision as a seal until the fulfillment of His promise in the New Testament. In its due time, that promise was fulfilled when Jesus Christ came in the flesh and gave His life. From the time of the resurrection of the Lord Jesus, however, the signet ring's seal became internal. The Holy Spirit put His seal on the new heart of believers.

The Lord told Israel, "I will betroth you to me forever; I will betroth you in righteousness and justice, in love and compassion. I will betroth you in faithfulness, and you will acknowledge the LORD" (Hosea 2:19–20). In the New Testament, the apostle Paul told the Corinthian church something similar: "I am jealous for you with a godly jealousy. I promised you to one husband, to Christ, so that I might present you as a pure virgin to him" (2 Corinthians 11:2). A similar thing happens spiritually the day a person accepts the Lord Jesus Christ as their personal Savior. God places the seal of the Spirit, which is God's mark, on the individual's life (see Ephesians 1:13; 4:30). The hour the Lord Jesus is invited into our lives, the deposit of the Holy Spirit is given as a promise from God. At that moment, we are sealed with the Holy Spirit's seal for the day of salvation. One of the greatest verses about such a sealing is Ephesians 1:13–14. In these verses, the apostle Paul makes so clear the promise brought with the Holy Spirit's sealing:

> You also were included in Christ when you heard the
> message of truth, the gospel of your salvation. When

48

you believed, you were marked in him with a *seal*, the promised Holy Spirit, who is a deposit guaranteeing our inheritance until the redemption of those who are God's possession—to the praise of his glory.

Ephesians 1:13–14, emphasis added

Wow! What an engagement ring we have been given! In this Scripture, the Holy Spirit is referred to as a seal. That is the Lord's signature for the security of our redemption, as well as the intervention of the Lord Jesus Christ in our lives. This seal allows the Holy Spirit's healing to establish an eternal relationship between a believer and the Lord Jesus Christ. Furthermore, the seal of the Holy Spirit gives a believer full right and legal authority to become a child of God. The indwelling of the Holy Spirit starts at the moment the believer expresses a desire to know God, and it enables a believer to call on God. "Because you are his sons, God sent the Spirit of his Son into our hearts, the Spirit who calls out, 'Abba, Father'" (Galatians 4:6). As far as our salvation is concerned, nothing is greater than this.

> *"Because you are his sons, God sent the Spirit of his Son into our hearts, the Spirit who calls out, 'Abba, Father'" (Galatians 4:6). As far as our salvation is concerned, nothing is greater than this.*

Yet it still begs the question that if the day of engagement is this glorious, then what more will it be like on the day that the wedding of the Lamb takes place. Fortunately, John the Revelator provided us with a description of that powerful day.

I heard what sounded like a great multitude, like the roar of rushing waters and like loud peals of thunder, shouting: "Hallelujah! For our Lord God Almighty reigns. Let us rejoice and be glad and give him glory! For the wedding of the Lamb has come, and his bride has made herself ready. Fine linen, bright and clean, was given her to wear."

Revelation 19:6–8

What a day that will be when Jesus says to the Father, "Here is My Bride for whom I gave My life and whom I bought with My blood the day I said, 'This is My blood for the new covenant.'"

After this I looked, and there before me was a great multitude that no one could count, from every nation, tribe, people and language, standing before the throne and before the Lamb. They were wearing white robes and were holding palm branches in their hands. And they cried out in a loud voice: "Salvation belongs to our God, who sits on the throne, and to the Lamb."

Revelation 7:9–10

This was revealed when the Lord Jesus took the scroll and opened the book that no one else could open. When He broke the seal, there was a new song for the Bridegroom.

They sang a new song, saying, "You are worthy to take the scroll and to open its seals, because you were slain, and with your blood you purchased for God persons from every tribe and language and people and nation. You have made them to be a kingdom and priests to serve our God, and they will reign on the earth."

Revelation 5:9–10

Both in the Old Testament and the New Testament, the seal of God is always shown by the presence of God. All through the Old Testament, the Lord promised His people, who had accepted His covenant through cir-
cumcision, that He would be with them. He called them "My people." He was with them. He was for them. He dwelt among them through the Tabernacle and the Temple. His gra-cious hand was upon their leaders as a seal, His covenant. In the New Tes-tament, from the day the Holy Spirit sealed us for redemption, He is always in us and with us. That is why the apostle Paul said, "Do not grieve the Holy Spirit of God, with whom you were sealed for the day of redemption" (Ephesians 4:30). We carry the Holy Spirit's seal as a sign of His indwelling presence daily, until the day we see Him face-to-face. What an assurance of security and protection!

> *Even if a signet ring is sold, given away or stolen, it retains the covenant power of the original owner.*

The seal of the Lord is one of the greatest assurances we have concerning the presence of God and His loving care. Even if a signet ring is sold, given away or stolen, it retains the covenant power of the original owner. The owner has the right to restore the promises that go with it. Our identity is what gives us spiritual authority to live and act as children of God.

The Holy Spirit in us is representative of His signet ring, His covenant. The covenant demonstrates an agreement with the Lord and His covenant people in which the Lord forges a union to accomplish a common goal that fortifies His people in His Kingdom. Through the power of the Holy Spirit, we are able to achieve great and mighty things for His purposes.

When we understand His commitment to us with an unbreakable sign of covenant, how can we not choose to live for His glory and enjoy His peace and security? Our awareness of His presence and His everlasting mark on our lives increases with a greater intensity and spiritual desire to host His presence. We protect His presence daily by abiding in Him. Hence, this becomes not only a sure foundation but also an engine for an ongoing relationship with effective, fruitful ministry.

───────── SIGNET RING DECREES ─────────

In Jesus' name, I decree that

- *I receive the seal of the Holy Spirit on my life.*
- *I welcome Your presence daily.*
- *I walk in Your authority here on earth.*
- *I receive the restoration of Your promises.*
- *I choose to live for Your glory.*

3

Signet Rings as Symbols of Kingly Authority

Alemu Beeftu

Pharaoh said to Joseph, "I hereby put you in charge of the whole land of Egypt." Then Pharaoh took his signet ring from his finger and put it on Joseph's finger. He dressed him in robes of fine linen and put a gold chain around his neck. He had him ride in a chariot as his second-in-command, and people shouted before him, "Make way!" Thus he put him in charge of the whole land of Egypt.

Genesis 41:41–43

Once I heard a story told by my good friend. The parable went like this:

A king who ruled for many years was getting old. He decided to look for a successor to pass on the authority to rule the people. To find out the wise and faithful person among the young people, he decided to give them a test. The test was to give them seed and ask them to grow it and bring the fruit at the appointed time and show him. He gave each person seeds and a pot to grow them, and gave them enough time for the seed to grow and bear fruit.

On the appointed day, all his subjects were gathered to see whom the king would choose as the next king. Those who took seeds and a pot also gathered with great anticipation to win. Everybody brought amazing plants with fruits. They wanted to be a winner and become the next king, except for one young person who brought back an empty pot. The king inspected everybody's plant, including the person who brought the empty pot.

The king went back to his throne and said, "I have made my decision and have found a wise and faithful person who will become my successor." As everybody was waiting, he called out the young man with the empty pot and said he would be the next king.

Everybody was puzzled.

Then the king spoke. "I gave all of you cooked seeds that don't grow. You replaced what I gave you to win the kingship, except for this young man, who brought back an empty pot. Kingly authority is measured by faithfulness, and therefore he will be your king."

The testimony about Jesus, the Lord of lords and the King of kings, is, "He was faithful to the one who appointed him, just as Moses was faithful in all God's house" (Hebrews 3:2).

The primary responsibilities of Old Testament kings involved participation in religious rituals, managing the affairs of the state in war and peace, writing laws and guiding the administration and execution of justice. Kings were chosen by divine appointment. In addition to the signet ring, their authority symbols included the kingly garment, crown, anointing, scepter and throne.

The Kingly Garment

A garment is a sign of identity that signifies the office of the person wearing it and may be used to affirm a change of identity. Royal garments start with a royal mantle. When kings took office, they received a mantle as a symbol of authority. Special garments such as royal robes were used to distinguish individuals from others. Kingly garments affirm a person's legal authority to establish justice and to lead his subjects, while priestly garments were to separate priests for the service of God from others by establishing a new identity for new levels of relationship with God. We read about this garment of authority in biblical accounts.

Joseph's Garment

Joseph's garment of many colors is a good example. It separated him from his brothers by showing his father's special love and care. Joseph started dreaming after Jacob put the garment of many colors on him. The first thing his brothers did, before they sold him to the Egyptians, was to take off his garment, tear it and dip it in blood. They didn't like his dream and his garment. While his dream was an internal voice, the garment was the external sign of his prophetic destiny. When Joseph refused to sleep with Potiphar's wife, she took his garment to use it to accuse him. Both his brothers and Potiphar's wife used Joseph's garments as proof of their deceptive intentions and actions to destroy his life and character, to stop him from reaching his prophetic destiny.

The beauty of God's work is that all of this didn't stop Joseph, but when the hour of divine appointment arrived, he was rushed to become the second leader in authority with a new garment of power. After Pharaoah removed the signet ring from his own finger and gave it to Joseph to wear, "he dressed him in robes of fine linen and put a gold chain around his neck. He had him ride in a chariot as his second-in-command, and people shouted before him, 'Make way!' Thus he put him in charge of the whole land of Egypt" (Genesis 41:42–43).

Furthermore, whether Jacob bestowed it with prophetic insight, Joseph's garment was a prophetic picture of his life calling to be a leader to save others. After revealing his true identity to his family, Joseph himself made a declaration to his brothers. He "reassured them and spoke kindly to them," saying, "Don't be afraid. Am I in the place of God? You intended to harm me, but God intended it for good to accomplish what is now being done, the saving of many lives. So then, don't be afraid. I will provide for you and your children" (Genesis 50:21, 19–21).

We observe a similar thing in the ordination of high priests.

Aaron's Garment

The Lord told Moses before he ordained Aaron to put upon him a garment of dignity and honor as a sign of the authority of his office: "You are to make sacred garments [official clothing reserved for holy services] for Aaron your brother, for honor and for beauty" (Exodus 28:2 AMP). Hence, the garment of the high priest signified the following: (1) anointing (power and presence of God) to qualify to stand before Holy God with a garment of honor and beauty (see Isaiah 61:10) and (2) authority to declare the Living Word of God and pronounce the blessings of God. Such spiritual authority and identity enabled the high priests to enter into the presence of God, carrying the twelve tribes' names on His heart and shoulders (see Exodus 28:12, 29). This qualified him to establish a standard of holiness for standing before God. That was the reason why every high priest was anointed wearing the same garment (see Exodus 29:29). That was also the basis for Satan's accusation of Joshua, the great high priest (see Zechariah 3:3–4). In Joshua's defense, the Lord rebuked the enemy and closed the door to the accuser by removing his filthy garment and placing on him a new garment, clean turban and crowns of authority (see Zechariah 6:11).

The Kingly Crown

Crowns are ornamental headdresses worn by a monarch as a symbol of authority. Typically, they are made of precious metals and jewels. Crowns in the ancient world were made of very costly materials, symbolizing royalty and sovereignty, and were in various shapes and forms. Definitions of a crown include the crown as a symbol of war triumphs. It signifies the highest level of achievement. It can be an emblem of victory worn by athletes as a badge of honor and courage. Crowns are symbols of rewards of service—an insignia of accomplishment of power and authority.

Crowns are also a sign of kingly anointing. A crown is what separates a true king with full authority from another without authority. Once a king has a crown on his head, his power and authority are not challenged because of his public anointing. A crown is the final sign of legal authority that has resulted from anointing. Hence, it is to affirm identity with authority and position. A crown is, therefore, what separates the king from other siblings in the same bloodline since becoming a king is about bloodline.

A crown is a sign of identification, and that is why it is worn during ceremonial processions and at times of formal service, such as court, judgment or promotion. During his recent special message, Dr. Don Crum described this increased authority in the following way:

> Being around kings in Africa for many years as my family and I lived in Africa for eight years and still have a work there, I have noticed about kings: The crown they begin with is not the same crown they end their reign with. The crown takes new form and fashion throughout the reign. In other words, the crown they were coronated to wear at the beginning of their reign might not be as glorious as the crown they will end their reign with. They will add more beauty to a king's crown. Sometimes they will melt it down into gold, into that raw portion and form. Then refashion it into a more glorious crown, adding gold to it, the content of gold increasing, and even new jewels and precious gems of all kinds. That king, when he does mighty exploits for his nation or his tribe or his kingdom, this is what then qualifies him for an increase of crown authority both as he operates, but also what is upon his head as a significant sign of his authority. . . . God is adding layers just like in the old days. The kings, as they conquered enemy kings, would often take a portion of the conquered king's robe and add it to the robe of the king who conquered that king. So the king wears

an increase of authority, and his crown may change as well during his reign.[1]

In addition to being a sign of increased authority, a crown can also be used as a sign of a reward of victory or mark of honor.

Crowns in Bible imagery signify what the wearer has accomplished, conquered and gained rule over. The Kingdom of God is about the rulership of the King of kings, and the Bible mentions five different crowns by name: the incorruptible crown, the crown of rejoicing, the crown of righteousness, the crown of glory and the crown of life.

1. The Incorruptible Crown

As believers, Paul and Peter, the apostles, were encouraging the people of God to pursue their prize and inheritance through the power of the resurrection of Jesus Christ. All things on earth will decay and perish. Paul asked, "Do you not know that in a race all the runners run, but only one gets the prize?" Then he wrote, "Run in such a way as to get the prize. Everyone who competes in the games goes into strict training. They do it to get a crown that will not last, but we do it to get a crown that will last forever" (1 Corinthians 9:24–25; see 1 Peter 3:4).

2. The Crown of Rejoicing

In this world of much suffering and pain, we must keep our goal on the hope of Jesus Christ. We can rejoice in the hope He has given us. We can rejoice as we look to the future. "What is our hope, our joy, or the crown in which we will glory in the presence of our Lord Jesus when he comes? Is it not you? Indeed, you are our glory and joy" (1 Thessalonians

2:19–20). In Revelation 21:4, John wrote, "'He will wipe every tear from their eyes. There will be no more death' or mourning or crying or pain, for the old order of things has passed away."

3. The Crown of Righteousness

Our inheritance through Christ Jesus gives us His righteousness. It is an everlasting crown promised to all. Through the endurance of discouragements, persecutions, sufferings or even death, the reward is eternity in heaven with Christ. "Now there is in store for me the crown of righteousness, which the Lord, the righteous Judge, will award to me on that day—and not only to me, but also to all who have longed for his appearing" (2 Timothy 4:8).

4. The Crown of Glory

This crown is rewarded to all who long for His appearing. The crown of glory refers to God's nature and His actions. When Stephen was stoned, he looked to heaven and saw the splendor and brightness (see Acts 7:54–60). Our life on earth cannot even be compared to the coming glory. Peter wrote, "Be shepherds of God's flock that is under your care, watching over them. . . . And when the Chief Shepherd appears, you will receive the crown of glory that will never fade away" (1 Peter 5:2, 4).

5. The Crown of Life

Jesus Christ provides what is required in our spiritual lives. He provides living water, and He is the Bread of Life. Our earthly lives end, but we have the incredible promise of eternal life. As the children of God, we are to look forward. He is the Author and Finisher of our faith. "Blessed is the one who perseveres under trial because, having stood the test, that person will receive the crown of life that God has promised to those who love him" (James 1:12). In the end, when we place our crowns at His feet, there will be robes and other precious mantles to reflect the glory and authority of the King of kings.

> Whenever the living creatures give glory, honor and thanks to him who sits on the throne and who lives for ever and ever, the twenty-four elders fall down before him who sits on the throne and worship him who lives for ever and ever. They lay their crowns before the throne and say: "You are worthy, our Lord and God, to receive glory and honor and power, for you created all things, and by your will they were created and have their being."
>
> Revelation 4:9–11

As believers, our calling is to move from glory to glory. The Lord is refashioning it for the future, because the crown we have worn in the past will not be sufficient to take us into the battle, given the victory that we are heading into now as His people.

The Kingly Anointing

The Lord commissioned a king by anointing his head with anointing oil publicly: "I have found David my servant; with my sacred oil I have anointed him" (Psalm 89:20). The Lord told Samuel to go and anoint David to replace King Saul. That anointing established an incredibly special relationship between David and God. "He will call out to me, 'You are my Father, my God, the Rock my Savior.' And I will appoint him to be my firstborn, the most exalted of the kings of the earth" (vv. 26–27). David lived many years, however, after he was anointed by Samuel before he wore the crown and was seated on his throne.

In Isaiah 45:1, the Lord promised to activate His power and presence, the result and sign of true anointing. Leaders who were called, anointed and carried His seal received the Holy Spirit's power to do His will both in the Old and New Testaments. Here are a few examples:

- Gideon: "Then the Spirit of the LORD came upon Gideon" (Judges 6:34).
- Saul: "The Spirit of the LORD will come powerfully upon you" (1 Samuel 10:6). "When [Saul] and his servant arrived at Gibeah, a procession of prophets met him; the Spirit of God came powerfully upon him, and he joined in their prophesying" (v. 10). "The Spirit of God came powerfully upon [Saul], and he burned with anger" (11:6).
- David: "Samuel took the horn of oil and anointed him in the presence of his brothers, and from that day on the Spirit of the LORD came powerfully upon David" (1 Samuel 16:13).
- Jesus: "God anointed Jesus of Nazareth with the Holy Spirit and power" (Acts 10:38). "Jesus returned to Galilee in the power of the Spirit" (Luke 4:14).
- The apostles: "You will receive power when the Holy Spirit comes on you" (Acts 1:8).
- Paul: "By the power of signs and wonders, through the power of the Spirit of God" (Romans 15:19).

Becoming a king is not about vote but about bloodline. A dynasty is formed when a person becomes a king not because of election but because of bloodline. One dictionary defines the word *dynasty* as "a succession of rulers of the same line of descent."[2]

David is called the firstborn because from that day forward David was expected to function in the fully delegated authority of God on earth to serve God's purpose and His people. When a king is anointed, therefore, he is given delegated power to walk in full authority to do the kingdom's work. God promised David, among other things, to sustain him, strengthen him, judge his enemies, exalt his horn (increase his power), give him victory, maintain His love for him and keep His covenant with him. That is the resulting anointing.

> *Becoming a king is not about vote but about bloodline.*

The authority of God is not fixed all the years of our lives. We get promoted in our lives and ministries to higher levels of authority, so the authority we begin with is not the same level that we end with. Missions and assignments become more impactful in the nations, and there is a need for an increase of authority. That's what I call operational authority. That comes by the anointing of the Spirit of the Lord. Just as we have talked in the past about authority, there is authority by position just like a civil government ruler moves into a position of authority. Civil servants have authority by virtue of operating out of their positions, but there is a different authority that God works with that is called authority by anointing.

David, for example, was anointed by the Lord through the prophet Samuel to be the next king of Israel. Samuel didn't pour the fullness of that anointing onto David, however, nor did the Lord do that at that time. Samuel gave David the first portion of what would later become three portions of a kingly anointing. Fourteen years later, David, after receiving the first kingly anointing, became a king over Judah, which was a portion of Israel. At that time, he received his second kingly anointing and commission to become king of Judah. Later, he became king over all of Israel and received his third and final anointing to rule and govern over the entire nation of Israel.

The Lord is especially wise in that He does not give us the fullness of a king's anointing at the beginning, but He gives us a portion, and we prove ourselves faithful in that portion. After that, He qualifies us for an additional increased portion of a kingly anointing. God increases kingly authority through relationship (chapter 8) and service to build our character.

- Serving increases our impact.
- Serving is the test of true authority and power.
- Serving is a reflection of the heart and an indicator of true character.
- Serving is recognizing the Source of true authority.
- Serving is the best way to become mature.
- Serving is the best way of training others.
- Serving is a sign of love.
- Serving is a sign of true humility.
- Serving shows our true values.

A king's primary authority is in his anointing. That is why the Lord Jesus, the King of kings, started His ministry by declaring, "The Spirit of the Lord is on me, because he has anointed me" (Luke 4:18). The anointed King has full authority to delegate power to those who represent Him and to carry out the interests of His Kingdom. Jesus gave power to His disciples (you and me) when He proclaimed, "I have given you authority to trample on snakes and scorpions and to overcome all the power of the enemy; nothing will harm you" (Luke 10:19). This is walking in the kingly anointing.

The King's Scepter

The scepter, which the ancient kings of the East usually had with them, had its origin in the shepherd's rod. Kings were considered to be shepherds of their people. Thus, the scepter, or rod, of the king became a symbol of protection, power and authority. The king's scepter is a symbol of sovereignty that includes autonomy, freedom, independence, liberty and so forth. "Shepherd your people with your staff, the flock of your inheritance" (Micah 7:14). David mentions the staff along with the rod when he walks through the valley of death (see Psalm 23:4).

A staff is a stick measuring five or six feet long and sometimes, but not always, has a crook at the end of it. It is used as people in Western countries would use a cane or walking stick. It is useful in handling sheep and for protection. From early times, a staff, rod or scepter has been a symbol of either secular or religious authority. In modern times it is quite often used as a decorative symbol for ceremonies. In the Old Testament, the scepter originated as the ruler was a shepherd of his people. An official uses the scepter to exercise the necessary authority to care for the flock.

The Bible describes the authority of the Lord over kings, peoples and nations. The scepter was used as a symbol of God's rule. This psalm is significant because it also applies to Jesus: "Your throne, O God, will last for ever and ever; a scepter of justice will be the scepter of your kingdom" (Psalm 45:6). Scripture records the relationship with Christ and how we are united with Him and sharing in the Spirit (see Philippians 2:1–18). In our relationships with other people, as believers, we have the same mindset as Christ Jesus.

The apostle Paul used a phrase about the possibility of coming with a rod in a strong way to give guidance. The rod is used in Scripture as a symbol of God's authority, laws and commandments. The term *rod* or *iron*, therefore, speaks to us about being bound to God's authority, laws and commandments. "For the kingdom of God is not a matter of talk but of power. What do you prefer? Shall I come to you with a rod of discipline, or shall I come in love and with a gentle spirit?" (1 Corinthians 4:20–21).

One purpose for a rod was in measurement, but rods also were used as symbols of authority, as staffs and for correction and punishment. Scepters were in some measure often considered rods as well as the staffs of shepherds. Kings extend the scepter of authority to show mercy and favor. Finally, the scepter is given by the king to authorize individuals, according to the faithfulness of the individual.

The Kingly Throne

A throne is a chair occupied by a high-ranking official, such as a monarch or cleric of high order, as an archbishop or a bishop, a church dignitary. It is a symbol of distinction for state or ceremonial occasions. A throne is a seat of authority to rule and administer justice. In the relationship regarding a king, it signifies royal power and dignity. A king's throne is about his dominion, rulership, power, majesty and full control. Frequently, it is placed on a dais and sometimes has a canopy and ornate decoration. The person who sits on the throne has power and dignity.

When the Bible speaks of God's throne, the emphasis is on God's dignity and sovereign rule. The fact that His throne is in heaven further emphasizes the divine nature of God's existence. The New Testament is a continuation of the Jewish identification of heaven as the throne of God. Located in heaven, it also has a secondary seat at the right hand of God, where Christ sits. Even though we are in desperate situations with enemies and wars surrounding us that we cannot control, God has given His promise. He is sovereign, and He rules and reigns. "LORD Almighty, the God of Israel, enthroned between the cherubim, you alone are God over all the kingdoms of the earth. You have made heaven and earth" (Isaiah 37:16).

Whenever living creatures give glory, honor and thanks to Him who sits on the throne and who lives forever and ever, the 24 elders fall down before Him who sits on the throne and worship Him who lives forever and ever.

> At once I was in the Spirit, and there before me was a throne in heaven with someone sitting on it. And the one who sat there had the appearance of jasper and ruby. A rainbow that shone like an emerald encircled the throne. Surrounding the throne were twenty-four other thrones, and seated on them were twenty-four elders. They were dressed in white and had crowns of gold on their heads.
>
> Revelation 4:2–4

They lay their crowns before the throne, announcing, "You are worthy, our Lord and God, to receive glory and honor and power, for you created all things, and by your will they were created and have their being" (v. 11). John continued,

> Then I saw a Lamb, looking as if it had been slain, standing at the center of the throne, encircled by the four living creatures and the elders. The Lamb had seven horns and seven eyes, which are the seven spirits of God sent out into all the earth. He went and took the scroll from the right hand of him who sat on the throne. . . . Then I saw a great white throne and him who was seated on it. The earth and the heavens fled from his presence, and there was no place for them. And I saw the dead, great and small, standing before the throne, and books were opened. Another book was opened, which is the book of life. The dead were judged according to what they had done as recorded in the books. The sea gave up the dead that were in it, and death and Hades gave up the dead that were in them, and each person was judged according to what they had done. Then death and Hades were thrown into the lake of fire. The lake of fire is the second death. Anyone whose name was not found written in the book of life was thrown into the lake of fire.
>
> 5:6–7; 20:11–15

Compare this with Hebrews 4:6, which says, "It still remains for some to enter that rest, and since those who formerly had the good news proclaimed to them did not go in because of their disobedience."

In the natural, a monarch doesn't share his or her throne. They usually delegate authority with responsibility, but they don't give up their throne, since that is the final sign of power. This is different, however, with the King of kings and Lord of lords, the King Jesus Christ. He paid the price for our sins to free us from being slaves to sin and made us kings and priests to God the Father (see Revelation 1:5–6). Every child of God has received authority to rule and reign with King Jesus Christ. "God raised us up with Christ and seated us with him in the heavenly realms in Christ Jesus" (Ephesians 2:6).

Every child of God has received authority to rule and reign with King Jesus Christ.

In summary, the kingly garment, crown, anointing, scepter and throne were all symbols of honor, but nothing held the power and authority like that of the signet ring. It was the final symbol and signature of the king for documents, laws, decrees, legal matters and so on of that day.

The primary responsibilities of Old Testament kings involved participation in religious rituals, managing the affairs of the state in war and peace, writing laws and guiding the administration and execution of justice. Kings were chosen by divine appointment. In addition to the signet ring, their authority symbols included the kingly garment, crown, anointing, scepter and throne.

Although the signet ring was the true symbol of authority, used throughout the kingdom by the king, even replacing his signature at times, the other kingly items, like his garment, crown, scepter and throne, still gave the position the honor and superiority it deserved. The signet ring alone is what truly carried the weight and authority of the king's full reign and power.

——————— **SIGNET RING DECREES** ———————

In Jesus' name, I decree that

- *I now receive a new garment of authority, sealing my new identity in You.*
- *I now receive a crown of kingly authority from You.*
- *I now receive a kingly anointing, along with Your power and presence.*
- *I now receive a kingly scepter as a symbol of Your protection, power and authority.*
- *I now receive my seat in heavenly places with You, King Jesus.*

PART II

SIGNET RINGS IN
Ancient Israel

4

The First
Biblical Mentions
of the Signet Ring

ALEMU BEEFTU

"With work like a jeweler engraves on a *signet*, you are
to inscribe the two stones with the names of the sons
of Israel, and you are to mount them in settings of gold
filigree. . . . The stones are to correspond to the names of
the sons of Israel, twelve stones corresponding to their
names. They are to be engraved like a signet, each with
the name of one of the twelve tribes."

Exodus 28:11, 21 ISV, emphasis added

As previously discussed, a signet ring is a seal that
carries the king's signature. So what is the Hebrew
word that translates as "seal," "signet" or signet

ring?"[1] In *Strong's* there are three words that relate to the word *signet*. Two are in Hebrew; one is Aramaic in origin. They are as follows:

- *H2368:* חותם חתם (*chowtham*), *meaning "signet, seal"*
- H2858: חתמת (*chothemeth*), meaning "signet"
- H5824: עזקא (*`izqa'*) Aramaic word, meaning "signet"

Of the 23 occurrences of the word *signet* in eleven translations of the Bible,[2] the first time a signet ring is mentioned in the Bible is in Genesis, the first book in the Bible. The first five books of the Old Testament (Genesis, Exodus, Leviticus, Numbers and Deuteronomy) are called the Pentateuch.[3] This chapter explores the origin, uses and significance in these early books of the Hebrew Scriptures.

Judah

Genesis 29:35 tells us that Judah, whose name means "praise" in Hebrew, was the fourth son that Leah bore for Jacob.[4] Judah married Shua, and their firstborn was a son called Er. But the Lord killed Er because of his wickedness. His brother Onan became the kinsman to raise offspring with Er's wife, Tamar. But Onan knew that any child he fathered biologically wouldn't be his heir, "so whenever he slept with his brother's wife, he spilled his semen on the ground to keep from providing offspring for his brother. What he did was wicked in the LORD's sight; so the LORD put him to death also" (38:9–10). Judah sent Tamar home to live with her father by promising her that once his son Shelah grew up, he would marry her. But Judah didn't keep his promise because Shelah died.

One day, Tamar was told that her father-in-law was passing through the town. She disguised herself as a prostitute and approached Judah, whose wife had died. When he asked her to sleep with him, she said to him, "What will you give me to sleep with me?" Judah then asked, "What pledge should I give you?" and Tamar replied, "Your *seal* and its cord, and the staff in your hand" (Genesis 38:18 NIV, emphasis added). In another translation, verse 18 says: "Thy signet, and thy bracelets, and thy staff that is in thine hand" (KJV). Even more significantly, that verse in the International Standard Version reads, "Your signet ring, cord, and the staff in your hand." Judah agreed to send her a young goat, his signet ring and a cord and staff as a pledge until she received the goat. Yet when he sent the goat, the messenger could not find the harlot that Judah described and so could not retrieve Judah's belongings.

Three months later, Judah heard Tamar had become pregnant by way of harlotry. Unable to put two and two together and realize the child was his, he gave the order for his men to burn her for her broken vow. But as they were taking her to her death, she sent the signet ring to Judah saying, "I am pregnant by the man who owns these. . . . See if you recognize whose seal and cord and staff these are'" (v. 25).

It is worth noting that Judah convinced his brothers not to kill Joseph and instead sell him to Midianite slave traders (see Genesis 37:26–27).[5] And we now turn our attention to Joseph's story.

Joseph and Pharaoh's Signet Ring

The second time a signet ring is mentioned in the Bible is when Pharaoh extended his signet ring to Joseph.[6] Though he was a slave, Joseph was the first person in the Old Testament to receive Pharaoh's signet ring to save nations. Joseph was the ninth son of Jacob and the first child of Rachel. He was born after many anguished prayers. At one point, because of Rachel's pain, she said to Jacob, "Give me children, or I'll die!" (Genesis 30:1). This was the depth of her pain over being unable to bear a child. But God, in His mercy, heard her prayer and blessed her with Joseph. "God remembered Rachel; he listened to her and enabled her to conceive. She . . . gave birth to a son and said, 'God has taken away my disgrace.' She named him Joseph, and said, 'May the LORD add to me another son'" (vv. 22–24).

Joseph was not born to be an answer to Rachel's prayers but was born to be an answer to nations that would suffer from famine in the distant future. Joseph was loved by his father, Jacob, more than all his brothers and sister. Not only was Joseph the son of Rachel, the wife he loved, but Jacob saw something exceptional in Joseph. As we observe from the blessing of his sons at the end of his life, Jacob was a prophet. "Jacob called for his sons and said: 'Gather around so I can tell you what will happen to you in days to come'" (Genesis 49:1).

In the case of Joseph, I believe Jacob saw the plan of God in Joseph's life. He saw that Joseph would be fruitful; that he would be attacked, but victorious; that God's help and blessings would be with him; and that he would be the prize among his brothers (see vv. 22–26). Because of this prophetic insight, Jacob loved Joseph more than his brothers and kept him at home with him. He also separated him from his brothers by placing upon him a garment of many colors, different from his other sons' garments. Amazingly, when his father put the garment of many colors on him, Joseph started dreaming. A garment is a picture of identity and an acceptance of love, covering and protection. The garment was a symbol of the security of knowing his father's love, which created in him the confidence to dream and share his dreams.

One day Jacob sent Joseph to his brothers with supplies they needed. Checking on his brothers' well-being and providing for them was part of his calling from the beginning. But his brothers didn't like him, so they bound him and sold him into slavery. Joseph was taken to Egypt as a slave, but there he became a leader, just as he had seen in his dream. The Lord took Joseph through a long character-building journey to qualify him to be trusted to wear Pharaoh's signet ring and ultimately save nations.

The enemy tried to kill Joseph because of the purpose and the call of God on his life. The enemy even used Joseph's own brothers to stop the fulfillment of Joseph's dream. When Joseph's brothers saw him coming, they said: "Here comes that dreamer! . . . Come now, let's kill him and throw him into one of these cisterns and say that a ferocious animal devoured him. Then we'll see what comes of his dreams" (37:19–20).

Rather than kill him, they decided to sell him as a slave. So began Joseph's journey of qualification under the hand of God. The first stop in this journey was Potiphar's house. Potiphar was the captain of the guard for Pharaoh. At Potiphar's house, the Lord proved that His call would not be stopped. The Lord's presence with Joseph, blessing the work of his hands and releasing special favor upon him, was evident and powerful. Potiphar quickly saw that the Lord was with Joseph, and he made him his personal attendant.

The second stop on Joseph's journey of qualification was an Egyptian prison. He was sentenced to prison because

Potiphar's wife made false accusations against him. First, Joseph's brothers had tried to destroy his dream by selling him and taking his garment of many colors—his true identity. Now, at Potiphar's house, Potiphar's wife aimed to destroy his character by approaching him for a sexual relationship. When he refused her demand, she accused him of rape, and he was put in prison.

Joseph's third stop was the prison cell. The presence of the Lord left Potiphar's house and went into the prison with Joseph. "While Joseph was there in the prison, the LORD was with him; he showed him kindness and granted him favor in the eyes of the prison warden" (39:20–21). The warden set Joseph in charge of the prison. But God used that prison as a testing ground to qualify him for his final assignment. "Joseph [was] sold as a slave. They bruised his feet with shackles, his neck was put in irons, till what he foretold came to pass, till the word of the LORD proved him true" (Psalm 105:17–19). He was tested until the appointed time of the Lord appeared. That appointed time came when Pharaoh had a dream.

Earlier, Joseph had interpreted dreams for two prisoners. One of the prisoners was Pharaoh's cupbearer, who was restored to his position according to Joseph's interpretation of his dream. Joseph asked him for help by presenting his case to Pharaoh: "When all goes well with you, remember me and show me kindness; mention me to Pharaoh and get me out of this prison" (Genesis 40:14). But the cupbearer forgot Joseph after he was restored to his position. Then Pharaoh started looking for an interpreter for two dreams he had. That was the Lord's appointed time. The Lord kept Joseph in prison to release him at the right moment and give him the signet ring of authority. Joseph's desire was to be freed from the prison, but God's plan was to place him in a position to rule Egypt, rescue people from starvation and save lives. I have witnessed this in my own life.

I was born and grew up in the countryside. I didn't know what God had preplanned for my life as I grew up. In fact, I didn't even know who God was in my early years. But I was always a curious child, even when I was helping my father with farming. Occasionally, a government-issued letter made its way to our family farm. One day I asked my father, "What is this thing you carry? Why does it make you look for someone?"

Joseph's desire was to be freed from the prison, but God's plan was to place him in a position to rule Egypt, rescue people from starvation and save lives.

My father answered, "I need someone who can tell me what is written on it." I responded, "What do I need to do to help you?"

My father replied, "You would learn how to read." I told him that I would love to do that. He said, "Since you are the last child, I need your help and cannot afford to send you to such a place." That was the day I saw a glimpse of my prophetic destiny—the promise of hope and a future. One day my mother's sister came to visit us at just the right time. During my aunt's visit, I learned about a school, Serving in Missions, which was five to six hours' walk from my home, but only four miles from her home. I was so excited about the school—even though I didn't have a clue what school was or looked like. I asked my aunt to let me go with her and find out what school looked like for myself.

The circumstances were stacked against me. I was a mere farm boy. I had no money. My parents were against my learning anything apart from farming, and that meant farming as it had been done for generations. I suggested to her that I could hide from my parents, wait for her in a field and go home with her to see the school. Then I would return home the next day. Because my appeal was so strong and heartfelt, she agreed.

The next day, I left home very early, waited for my aunt in the field and joined her on her journey home. For me, this was my first step into the unknown, the first step of my breakout for breakthrough. I respected my parents, yet I was compelled to take this step away from home. The walk to my aunt's house was the longest journey I had ever taken from home and from what I was familiar with. On that day, I took the journey of a lifetime, walking away from everything I knew, away from what I was expected to do and be. Without knowing its full implication, I took a first step of faith toward my prophetic destiny.

After more than a half-day journey with my aunt, we arrived at her house. That night was the first night I had ever spent outside of my home. The next day she told me how to get to the school. I had to cross a river near her home, then look for a big compound that was fenced with wire. She said, "The houses have tin roofs and that will be a sign for you. When you see the tin roofs, that is the school where children learn how to read and write. You will tell me what you think before you go back to your parents."

I had never seen a house with a tin roof before, so I didn't know what to look for. But I found the compound and entered through a big gate. I looked for children, but I didn't see any. I didn't realize that it was the middle of the "school year" and the children were in "classrooms." Two things I knew absolutely nothing about!

I kept looking around for someone. Finally, I saw a small office with the door halfway open. When I looked inside, I saw something else I had never seen before—a woman with a white face! I had always assumed everybody looked the same as me. My steep learning curve had already begun. I had never known that people could have different skin colors.

The white woman I saw in the office was the missionary director of the school. She spoke to me in Amharic, but I didn't understand her. I tried speaking my own language, and I gestured with my hands. I was desperate to tell her that I wanted to learn to read and write, and she saw my desperation. She gave me a sign to wait. She went away and brought back a teacher who spoke Oromigna.

After the woman heard my story, she was silent for several minutes—just looking at me. It was like an eternity to me because of my desperation. As she looked at me, I believe the woman saw the passion that had brought me there, in spite of poverty, distance and a lack of learning. She knew that I would need to learn Amharic quickly, and the school year was already half over. But I believe this opened her eyes to see determination, potential and the call of God on my life because of the favor and the grace of God. I believe that whether she knew it or not, she realized my prophetic destiny. This woman, who didn't know me, but who saw something in me, made a risky decision that day. She said to the teacher who was interpreting, "Take him to first grade."

When the director told me to follow the teacher to the classroom, she was as surprised as I was. She was violating two school policies—to admit students only at the beginning of the school year, and to admit only students who could speak Amharic. I never knew how she justified her decision or what repercussions she may have experienced for admitting me, but I am here today because of her decision many years ago. Perhaps she was simply fulfilling her God-given assignment as a missionary to Ethiopia. She trusted me with untested potential.

I don't know if that woman authored any books during her lifetime, but by admitting me into that school, she became something like a co-author for the more than forty books I have written. I don't know if she led thousands of people to the Lord, but because of what she did in my life, thousands of people receive the Lord every year through the ministry of Gospel of Glory. I don't know if she traveled around the world, but she has traveled through me to more than 54 nations on six continents, all because of one tremendous act of faith. She didn't only obey His voice, but she trusted me with the opportunity she gave me.

I never knew how she justified her decision or what repercussions she may have experienced for admitting me, but I am here today because of her decision many years ago.

And back to Joseph's story . . .

Pharaoh had heard about Joseph and his ability to interpret dreams. "Pharaoh sent for Joseph, and he was quickly brought from the dungeon. When he had shaved and changed his clothes, he came before Pharaoh" (Genesis 41:14). Joseph was brought to Pharaoh to interpret his dreams because his wise men were not able to interpret for him. The king needed Joseph because of his gift of interpretation, but God had brought him to Egypt with a divine strategy to lead a nation and to make provision for His covenant people as well as other nations. God filled him with knowledge, wisdom, understanding, discernment, vision and practical strategy.

After Joseph told Pharaoh the meaning of his dreams, there was an urgency that Pharaoh didn't yet understand. Joseph was able to give Pharaoh what the leader needed the most but didn't know to ask for—a strategy to save Egypt by maximizing the coming seven years of abundance. Joseph shared prophetic insight that went far beyond interpreting the king's dream. He told Pharaoh what the Lord would do and how soon and how firmly God had decided. And, to that prophetic insight, Joseph added a practical strategy for what ought to be done and who should do it. After he heard these things, Pharaoh made a declaration immediately that there was no better person to oversee this strategy than Joseph, who had the Spirit of God. He gave Joseph full authority instantly, including the signet ring from his own finger.

> Pharaoh said to Joseph, "I hereby put you in charge of the whole land of Egypt." Then Pharaoh took his *signet ring* from his finger and put it on Joseph's finger. He dressed him in robes of fine linen and put a gold chain around his neck. He had him ride in a chariot as his second-in-command, and people shouted before him, "Make way!" Thus he put him in charge of the whole land of Egypt.
>
> Genesis 41:41–43, emphasis added

Pharaoh's transfer of his ring from his finger to Joseph's was a symbol to show his promise of vesting him with royal authority. Rings are symbols of fully delegated authority. Pharaoh freely extended his signet ring, because he fully trusted Joseph.

Now remember, he trusted Joseph because of what he saw in Joseph—wisdom, knowledge, vision, understanding, caring for the well-being of his nation and kingdom. Pharaoh realized that he could trust Joseph. Pharaoh obviously knew that Joseph had a relationship with our God, and there was no one like him. That was the reason why he said, "Can we find anyone like this man, one in whom is the spirit of God?" (v. 38). After Pharaoh gave Joseph his signet ring, when people came to him with questions and needs, he simply said, "Go to Joseph and do what he tells you" (v. 55). He had delegated his authority to Joseph by giving him his signet ring. He couldn't do much without his signet ring. The signet ring had the seal of his authority. Hence, a king can give his signet ring to the person he trusts, and he can extend his scepter to a person he would like to have mercy upon, but he could not give away his crown and throne. That was the reason why Pharaoh said, "Only with respect to the throne will I be greater than you" (v. 40).

If Pharaoh could go this far, can you imagine the level of authority the Lord Jesus Christ has entrusted to us with the work of His Kingdom and meet the needs of this generation? You have the signet ring from the King of kings and the Lord of lords. "I saw the Lord seated on a throne, high and exalted, and the train of his robe filled the temple" (Isaiah 6:1 NIV1984).

Pharaoh didn't know Joseph's leadership and management skills, but because of the favor and the Spirit of God upon him, he saw the potential and gave him the signet ring as a sign of full authority.

Pharaoh confirmed Joseph's appointment and full authority over the land of Egypt by putting his signet ring on Joseph's finger. What a picture!

Joseph used the authority he was given through the signet ring to righteously govern the land of Egypt and nearby nations, including his own brothers and the rest of his family members. The day Pharaoh took off his signet ring and placed it on Joseph's finger, all authority was transferred to him. He used it with a pure heart and motive, clear vision, the highest level of integrity of character, unquestionable faithfulness to Pharaoh, great leadership and management skills and a compassionate, forgiving heart.

In Egypt, the signet ring of Pharaoh was proof of his divinity, claiming that he was the son of a particular god. According to Hebraic traditions, Joseph would not have been a son of a god, but the son of Jacob, chosen by God. Joseph's father, "the Mighty One, Jacob," had established his authority before God almighty. In other words, the biblical tradition refers to Jacob in near-divine terms and declares that he is God's chosen one. His son Joseph was selected by Pharaoh and given Pharaoh-like status.

The Lord had been preparing Joseph all along life's journey for such a time as this. Each of us has been given a signet ring from the King of kings and the Lord of lords for our sphere of influence. Our signet ring is established through our covenant relationship with Jesus Christ. Our promises are recorded in the Bible. Our Lord has a plan and purpose for us in His Kingdom. The question is, how well are we prepared to be used by God to save a generation?

Moses

Moving on to the second book in the Pentateuch, Moses was prepared by God in an exceptionally unusual way to be a chosen servant of the Lord. A number of indicators show that he was used as a signet ring on the Lord's hand to deliver God's people. The Lord did everything according to Moses' word and action. The Lord was with him as he spoke, and He taught him (see Exodus 4:12). His word shook the powerful kingdom of Egypt without any military power, with only his staff in his hand. God transformed Moses' staff into the rod that the Lord used with ultimate authority to perform signs and wonders in Egypt: dividing the Red Sea and bringing water from a rock. God spoke to Moses face-to-face, and in addition, Moses was in God's presence for forty days and nights. He reflected the glory and likeness of God. He received the Living Word of God in writing from the hand of God. He received the pattern from the Lord and built the Tabernacle, which was filled with the glory of God and became the standard for worship and approaching God.

Here are a few examples of where the signet ring is mentioned in the book of Exodus:

"You are to make a medallion of pure gold, and engrave on it 'Holy to the LORD,' like the engravings of a signet."

28:36 ISV

Then all whose hearts moved them, both men and women, came and brought brooches, earrings or nose rings, signet rings, and necklaces, all jewels of gold; everyone bringing an offering of gold to the LORD.

35:22 AMP

They prepared the onyx stones, engraved with the names of the sons of Israel like the engraving on a signet, and mounted them in settings of gold filigree. . . . The stones corresponded to the names of the sons of Israel, twelve stones corresponding to their names, with the engraving of a signet, each with the name of one of the twelve tribes.

39:6, 14 ISV

Moses prophesied about the coming of the Lord Jesus, "The LORD your God will raise up for you a prophet like me from among your own brothers" (Deuteronomy 18:15 CSB). The most important things in Moses' life and ministry were God's presence and glory. One of the strongest indications of becoming God's signet ring is to have a true desire to be in His presence and have His heart. Moses reflected God's heart through his humility and care for God's people. He was one of the first prophets in Israel, and we now turn our attention to other prophets, as well as high priests and kings, in the next chapter.

In summary, we have all been given gifts—signet rings—to fulfill God's purpose, not only in our own lives as a reflection of our identity but also our true authority to advance the work of His Kingdom. The question is, How will we use this authority? Will we use it for selfish gain as Judah did, or will we use it wisely as Joseph and Moses did? The important factor to remember is, we all have been given this choice: a responsibility to use our signet ring to help future generations. So it's highly recommended that we do all we can to protect these gifts—the signet rings God has given to us.

SIGNET RING DECREES

In Jesus' name, I decree that

- *the plans and purposes You have for my life will come to pass.*
- *You are now positioning me for favor.*

- *I now receive the full authority You are giving me.*
- *You will turn others' evil plans for my life for good.*
- *I will use the signet ring You are giving me to advance the work of Your Kingdom and help future generations.*

5

Kings, Prophets
and Priests

ALEMU BEEFTU

*Samuel took the horn of oil and anointed him in the
presence of his brothers, and from that day on the Spirit
of the LORD came upon David in power.*

1 Samuel 16:13 NIV1984

The signet ring is a sign of security and authority. The
Old Testament shows us occasions in which the Lord
selected and anointed individuals for three special offices with the full authority and protection of God to carry
out His eternal purposes on earth. In other words, the Lord
gave them the King's signet ring to do His will on earth.
These were the priestly, prophetic and kingly offices (see
illustration below).

High Priest
carrying the signet ring
to stand before God,
worship and pronounce
God's blessing.

Kings
given the signet ring
by the Lord of Hosts
to shepherd, lead,
protect, adminster
justice, etc.

Prophets
carrying the signet ring
of the Lord to speak the
word of the Lord and
release revelation for
correction and
direction.

The high priest was honored and protected by God because of His seal of anointing. The same is true with anointed kings. That was the reason why David refused to kill King Saul when he had opportunities to do so. "David said to Abishai, 'Don't destroy him! Who can lay a hand on the LORD's anointed and be guiltless?' . . . But the LORD forbid that I should lay a hand on the LORD's anointed" (1 Samuel 26:9, 11). The Bible records protection for prophets: "He allowed no one to oppress them; for their sake he rebuked kings: 'Do not touch my anointed ones; do my prophets no harm'" (1 Chronicles 16:21–22). The main reason for such care and protection was that they symbolically wore the Lord's signet ring. The high priest of the Lord was honored and protected by God. The apostle Paul was referring to this office when he said, "Brothers, I did not realize that he was the high priest; for it is written: 'Do not speak evil about the ruler of your people'" (Acts 23:5).

This chapter will discuss (1) how high priests carry the signet ring to stand before God, worship and pronounce God's blessing; (2) how kings are given the signet ring by the Lord of Hosts to shepherd, lead, protect, administer justice, etc.; and (3) how prophets carry the signet ring of the Lord to speak the word of the Lord and release revelation for correction and direction.

High Priests with the Signet Ring

The first office was that of the high priest, who was anointed to stand before the Lord to teach God's people. He pronounced God's blessings upon the people and offered daily sacrifices. He would also make atonement for the nation of Israel annually. The high priest was consecrated and anointed by God to function with full authority to pray for the people.

Aaron

The first one to be anointed and set apart with authority for the high priest's office was Aaron: "The LORD told Moses, . . . 'Make sacred garments for your brother Aaron to give him dignity and honor. . . . Take the anointing oil and anoint him by pouring it on his head'" (Exodus 25:1; 28:2; 29:7). And Moses "poured some of the anointing oil on Aaron's head and anointed him to consecrate him" (Leviticus 8:12).

Even before the anointing of ordination, the Lord told Moses to separate Aaron from others by making and placing upon him a special garment for beauty, dignity and separation from the rest. The four things that made Aaron's garment special were the robe, ephod, breastplate of judgment and the "miter," or upper turban. Hence, "the office, dress, and ministration of the high priest were typical of the priesthood of our Lord" (see Hebrews 4:14; 7:25; 9:12).[1]

The pouring of anointing oil on the priest's head was the final seal of approval to do his work with full authority. This act was the equivalent of giving a king his signet ring. The anointing was God's seal of approval, trust and security. According to biblical scholars, the high priest office, which started with Aaron, ended after a succession of 83 high priests in AD 70 with Phannias ben Samuel, an unrighteous priest who had no regard for the Lord.[2] In spite of the inconsistency of the high priests in the Old Testament, the Lord kept His promise: "I will raise up for myself a faithful priest, who will do according to what is in my heart and mind. I will firmly establish his priestly house, and they will minister before my anointed one always" (1 Samuel 2:35).

Joshua

Joshua was another person who became the Lord's signet ring. He knew divine order from the beginning through his submission to Moses. Joshua had a different spirit from those who rebelled against God. He challenged the assembly of Israel and led the people to the Jordan River. He marched around Jericho seven days. He fought the enemy and commanded the sun and the moon to stop by faith: "The sun stopped in the middle of the sky and delayed going down about a full day. *There has never been a day like it before or since, a day when the* LORD *listened to a human being.* Surely the LORD was fighting for Israel!" (Joshua 10:13–14, emphasis added).

Wow! What an authority and sign of a signet ring of the Lord of Hosts!

This reality was brought to light by what the Lord did for Joshua, the high priest in the Old Testament. Satan was bold enough to attack the identity of the high priest in the presence of the Lord. It is recorded in Zechariah 3:1, 3: "Then he showed me Joshua the high priest standing before the angel of the LORD, and Satan standing at his right side to accuse him. . . . Now Joshua was dressed in filthy clothes as he stood before the angel." Because of Joshua's filthy garment, Satan made an accusation against him to disqualify him from leading God's people as the high priest. Accusation is the action Satan always takes to condemn without truth and evidence. Satan's foremost goal is to disqualify God's children from a true and enjoyable relationship with God by attacking their identity, using past sin and iniquity. Opposition doesn't start with an attack on identity, but it builds toward an identity attack as the intensity of the shame of the past increases. Most of the time, false accusations start to spring up when a person is close to fulfilling their prophetic destiny. The Lord Jesus was accused falsely before He was crucified. Stephen was accused falsely before he was stoned. When false accusations are intensified, therefore, remember that you are remarkably close to fulfilling your calling.

In the case of Joshua, the basis for Satan's accusation was that he didn't have the typical high priestly garment that Aaron had. That garment gave him honor and beauty, as well as a new identity and authority to serve as high priest. Through this garment, the Lord also established a standard for holiness to stand before the Lord, worship, teach the people and declare blessings. From this time forward, every high priest was anointed wearing the same garment (see Exodus 29:29). During the captivity, however, everything that was in the Temple was destroyed or taken to Babylon. Joshua was the first high priest the Lord had chosen for the new Temple. Joshua came as he was. He was accepted by God as he was, just as the Prodigal Son was accepted by his father. When Satan accused him, Joshua didn't respond to the accusation or defend himself. But God, who called Joshua and brought him from the captivity to build the Temple and lead the people, came to his aid. First God rebuked Satan (see Zechariah 3:2). Then Joshua's filthy garments were removed, and he was given a new garment, again just as the Prodigal Son was given a new garment by his father. The most important thing for us to know is *where we are.* If we are in the presence of the Lord and in right relationship with Him, the Lord will be our defender. John wrote it this way: "My dear children, I write this to you so that you will not sin. But if anybody does sin, we have an advocate with the Father [one who speaks to the Father in our defense]—Jesus Christ, the Righteous One" (1 John 2:1).

The Lord shut the door on the accuser by giving Joshua a heavenly garment of righteousness that reflected the mercy of God and his new identity. His sin was forgiven, and the righteousness of God became his. The Lord renewed Joshua's mind and his thinking by placing a clean and righteous covering on his head. Even after forgiveness of sin, if our mind isn't renewed, we cannot walk in true identity with full spiritual authority. "This is what the LORD Almighty says: 'If you will walk in my ways and keep my requirements, then you will govern my house and have charge of my courts, and I will give you a place among these standing here'" (Zechariah 3:7 NIV1984). God entrusted Joshua with high spiritual authority, His house and all its affairs—as long as Joshua continued to walk with his God. Further, Joshua would have access to the presence of God, just as those he was standing among had.

Kings with Signet Rings

In 2019, a minuscule 2,600-year-old inscription was discovered in the City of David. The seal was deciphered by Dr. Anat Mendel-Geberovich of the Hebrew University of Jerusalem and the Center for the Study of Ancient Jerusalem. The rare seal impression from eighth century BCE had the name *Nathan-Melech* etched in it. It was discovered in an archaeological dig at the large Iron Age administrative center in Jerusalem's City of David. Nathan-Melech is named in 2 Kings as an official in the court of King Josiah. Archaeologist Dr. Yiftah Shalev of the Israel Antiquities Authority and Professor Yuval Gadot said, "The discovery of these two artifacts in a clear archaeological context that can be dated is very exciting."[3] The seal serves to connect the artifact and the actual physical era it was found in. This seal was found in the newly unearthed two-story public building, constructed with finely cut ashlar stones, and illustrates the beginning of a westward movement of the administrative area in the large sprawling city. The artifacts attest to the highly developed system of administration in the Kingdom of Judah and give considerable understanding of the economic status of Jerusalem as well as personal information about the king's closest officials and administrators. The seal and other artifacts demonstrate the covenants and belief systems in the eighth century.

Particularly in the context of God's people of covenant, the Jewish people, kings were set apart, designated and anointed as individuals and declared as high priests. The first king who received God's seal of approval and was anointed was King Saul. The people wanted a king like other nations around them, rather than the rulership or kingship of God over them. The Lord told Samuel He would send to him a man to anoint to govern the people. When Saul came to ask Samuel about lost donkeys, the Lord told him that Saul was the one. "Samuel took a flask of olive oil and poured it on Saul's head and kissed him, saying, 'Has not the Lord anointed you ruler over his inheritance?'" (1 Samuel 10:1). Samuel was referring to the calling and responsibility of the high priest's office when he said, "As for me, far be it from me that I should sin against the Lord by failing to pray for you. And I will teach you the way that is good and right" (12:23).

After that, as a sign of approval, the Spirit of God came upon King Saul in power, a sign of the signet ring of the God of Israel to govern His people. In the course of time, when King Saul disobeyed God, he lost God's approval, which was the equivalent of taking back the signet ring. He ruled Israel for many years without the presence and the voice of the Holy Spirit. He was governing without the king's signet ring. The one in possession of the king's signet ring was meant to do things according to the king's desire. King Saul had started using his authority to please people at the expense of obeying God.

The first time this occurred was when Saul made a burnt offering, because he didn't want to lose people. He was operating outside of God's direction and timing, and he knew it. Samuel told him that he had done a foolish thing. "Your kingdom will not endure; the Lord has sought out a man after his own heart and appointed him ruler of his people, because you have not kept the Lord's command" (13:14). That means the signet ring was taken from him. Instead of repenting and following the Lord, Saul used his position to please people again. When the Lord told him to entirely destroy the Amalekites, he kept the best animals to please the people. Samuel explained then how the Lord rejected Saul as king over Israel. The Lord took His signet ring and gave it to David by sending Samuel to anoint David. "The LORD said to Samuel, 'How long will you mourn for Saul, since I have rejected him as king over Israel? Fill your horn with oil and be on your way; I am sending you to Jesse of Bethlehem. I have chosen one of his sons to be king'" (16:1).

King David was given the signet ring to shepherd the people of God and to serve God's purpose. Samuel anointed him among his brothers. The Lord confirmed this commission: "I have found David my servant; with my sacred oil I have anointed him. . . . He will call out to me, 'You are my Father, my God, the Rock my Savior.' And I will appoint him to be my firstborn, the most exalted of the kings of the earth" (Psalm 89:20, 26–27). The Lord brought authority through the signet ring to the highest level by calling David His son instead of just His appointed king of Israel to replace King Saul. Wow! What power with the signet ring!

Using such authority, approval and security, David pleased God by correcting what went wrong during King Saul's rule. He brought back the Ark of His presence and His might. "Let us bring the ark of our God back to us, for we did not inquire of it during the reign of Saul" (1 Chronicles 13:3). David also made history by killing Goliath. No one had ever done such a thing before or after King David's reign. Furthermore, he shaped history by asking for and receiving a pattern from the Lord for the Temple and instructing his son Solomon to use the pattern in building the Lord's Temple in Jerusalem. David established a standard of excellence for all the kings who came after him. Every king was measured by King David's standard with a simple comparison: like his father David or *not* like his father David (see 2 Kings 21:21; 22:2).

Prophets with the Signet Ring

The third office that received the Lord's authority and approval was the office of the prophets because of their calling and relationship with God.

The First Prophets

Abraham was the first person called the Lord's prophet. He received God's calling, promises and protection, and he became a friend of God. The second person who established the true calling and standard of the prophet's office was Moses. He received a special calling from God and divine visitation. Moses closely walked with God, just like Abraham. God spoke to Moses face-to-face. The prophets were given the signet ring, as a sign of authority and approval to speak on the behalf of God. They gave guidance, brought correction, gave instruction, brought the presence of God and brought the word of God both for the present and the future. They would reveal the holiness of God, bring words of hope and restoration, pronounce God's judgment against sin and unfaithfulness and reveal God's heart and purposes. While priests preach and sing of God's mercy, prophets declare holiness and future hope through repentance. Among other things, the call of the prophet is to protect the holiness of God by speaking what they hear from God without adding to it or subtracting from it. One writer wrote, "The prophet stood before men, as a man who had been made to stand before God" (see 1 Kings 17:1; 18:15).[4]

Samuel

Samuel was given to the Lord at birth and set apart to serve the Lord. He grew up in the Temple and had favor with both

God and people. He started hearing the voice of the Lord as a child. From then on, the Lord continued to reveal Himself to Samuel. "The LORD was with Samuel as he grew up, and he let none of Samuel's words fall to the ground. And all Israel . . . recognized that Samuel was attested as a prophet of the LORD. The LORD . . . revealed himself to Samuel through his word" (1 Samuel 3:19–21). Surely, he became one of the Lord's signet rings among the people of Israel. He anointed both the first king of Israel and David, the king after God's own heart. Although the Lord sent Samuel to anoint David, Samuel became the Lord's signet ring. He said about David's anointing, "I have found David my servant; with my sacred oil I have anointed him" (Psalm 89:20). Yes, Samuel was the Lord's signet ring with full authority and great integrity of heart.

Elijah

Elijah was also used by the Lord as a signet ring. Elijah appeared in Israel when the spiritual condition of its people was at its worst, and they were suffering great persecution. The Israelites were hiding to survive. His primary calling was to bring back God's glory and demonstrate His power for others to see so that they might believe and return to God. When Elijah became a prophet, the spiritual foundation in Israel had been destroyed. Elijah described the spiritual condition of the nation: "I have been very zealous for the LORD God Almighty. The Israelites have rejected your covenant, broken down your altars, and put your prophets to death with the sword. I am the only one left, and now they are trying to kill me too" (1 Kings 19:10 NIV1984). When covenant has been broken and the fire of true worship is out, people cannot respond to the prophetic voice. The only way people in that spiritual condition can accept the prophets is if they choose to repent. When an individual, church or nation rejects God's voice, the judgment of God is at hand.

Elijah knew that God's judgment was at hand, and that was the reason he started his ministry on his knees in prayer. He asked the Lord to stop the rain until the nation understood the Source of their blessings. When God's people understood the Source, they would turn back to God. The Lord answered Elijah's fervent prayer by making him His signet ring. He closed the heavens and stopped the rain for three and a half years. Elijah's qualification came from his zealousness for the glory of the Lord. While he prayed in faith for the Lord to stop the rain, he also believed that the Israelites would know God as the true Source of all blessings. The Lord answered Elijah's prayer by giving him authority over nature in order to bring about the much-needed spiritual restoration. In other words, he became the Lord's signet ring. He used his authority without any hesitation. "As the Lord, the God of Israel, lives, whom I serve, there will be neither dew nor rain in the next few years except at my word" (17:1). The level of his authority was described by the phrase, *except at my word*.

After three and a half years, Elijah opened the heavens for rain by restoring the altar of worship. Once the altar is neglected and worship is compromised, the foundation is eroded. Once the altar of true worship is broken, the fire goes out. When the fire goes out, darkness takes over. There is no light! The enemy starts controlling, and the presence and glory of God depart. Then the Lord sent Elijah to bring restoration by rebuilding the old foundation of the Lord's broken altar.

Elijah decided to rebuild the old foundation even though he was alone. "Elijah said to all the people, 'Come here to me.' They came to him, and he repaired the altar of the LORD, which had been torn down" (18:30). After restoration of the altar and preparation of the sacrifice, Elijah prayed for the fire of God to return. God's fire fell and consumed the sacrifice, wood, stone, soil and water around the altar. This brought back not only the rain but also spiritual restoration, when people's hearts were turned back to God. "When all the people saw this, they fell prostrate and cried, 'The LORD—he is God! The LORD—he is God!'" (v. 39). This is true spiritual authority as a signet ring of the Lord.

The example of Elijah reveals key elements of the signet ring on the finger of God. These key elements are zeal for the glory of God, the prayer of faith, using spiritual authority appropriately, rebuilding the altar, doing everything according to the word of the Lord, praying for revival fire and focusing on returning the hearts of people to God.

Jezebel and the King's Signet Ring

Anything with a king's seal stamped on it was expected to be obeyed throughout his kingdom, since the seal was proof of a king's authority and power. Because of its authority, the king's signet ring could be used for both evil and noble purposes, much like any authority. The story of Jezebel and King Ahab provides a clear picture of how signet rings could be used with evil intention, to destroy or to kill.

Jezebel, the daughter of the king of Tyre, was a wife of King Ahab, a wicked king in Israel. Jezebel personified evil. A Phoenician princess, she led King Ahab into idol worship. During his reign, the spiritual condition of the nation was one of the evilest. The prophet Elijah summarized it when he responded, "I have been very zealous for the LORD God Almighty. The Israelites have rejected your covenant, torn down your altars, and put your prophets to death with the sword. I am the only one left, and now they are trying to kill me too" (19:10).

Because of Jezebel and Ahab, the Israelites committed many acts of disobedience against God, including three serious sins:

- First, they rejected the Lord's covenant, the same covenant the Lord made with their forefathers: Abraham, Isaac and Jacob. That covenant was what gave them their identity as a nation. Without the Lord's covenant, they had nothing. So Jezebel aimed to destroy their identity and the promises their fathers had received. Destroying identity and promises is always the evil one's target.

- They broke down the Lord's altar. In other words, she prevented the nation from worshiping the true God and led the nation into the worship of idols and false gods. This was the altar Elijah repaired before he prayed for the fire of God (see 1 Kings 18:30). When the Lord's altar is broken, worship is broken, and we lose our fire. Once the fire is out, the manifested glory of the Lord leaves. God's power and His presence are not in our midst. This was the primary strategy of the evil used by Jezebel in this case.

- They let their prophets die. By killing the prophets of God, Jezebel was trying to silence the voice of God and replace it with false prophets of Baal. Without God's prophets, the nation can't repent and seek the Lord for mercy. Without repentance, the Lord's judgment is unavoidable. Elijah knew he had to pray after he restored the altar of God: "Answer me, LORD, answer me, so

102

these people will know that you, LORD, are God, and that you are turning their hearts back again" (v. 37).

The desire of every true prophet is to turn people's hearts to God through repentance. Jezebel was the antithesis of that work. Jezebel was bent on using the king's signet ring for evil intentions.

One day, Ahab, Jezebel's husband, noticed a vineyard near his palace. He wanted to buy it and plant a vegetable garden. He asked the owner, Naboth the Jezreelite, to give or sell it to him. Naboth responded, "The LORD forbid that I should give you the inheritance of my ancestors" (21:3). Ahab went home disappointed and angry because of Naboth's refusal. When Jezebel asked why he was so sad, he told her about the vineyard. She told him that she would get the vineyard for him, though she didn't tell him how. Yes, it was the king's signet ring in the hand of the very evil Jezebel! She wrote a letter in Ahab's name and sealed it with his signet ring. The letter was written to the elders who lived in Naboth's village. He was to be accused falsely and killed in King Ahab's name, and it was sealed with the king's signet ring. "The elders and nobles who lived in Naboth's city did as Jezebel directed in the letters she had written to them" (v. 11). After that, she gave the vineyard to Ahab. This simple history shows the power a king's signet ring held during that era.

The desire of every true prophet is to turn people's hearts to God through repentance. Jezebel was the antithesis of that work. Jezebel was bent on using the king's signet ring for evil intentions.

Throughout the Old Testament, many have been God's signet ring with full authority. But the two individuals who were set apart as the Lord's signet ring in representing the Lord in the Old Testament were Moses and Elijah. They even appeared in the New Testament at the Mount of Transfiguration with the Lord Jesus Christ, representing the law and the prophets to seal the deal.

Prophets are approved by God to carry the seal of His approval. The instruction the apostle Paul gave to his spiritual son, Timothy, clearly describes the call and responsibility of the prophet's office and life: "Do your best to present yourself to God as one approved, a workman who does not need to be ashamed and who correctly handles the word of truth" (2 Timothy 2:15). In his writing to Thessalonian believers, Paul highlighted the responsibility of those who carry the signet ring or seal of God to do His will on earth: "On the contrary, we speak as those approved by God to be entrusted with the gospel. We are not trying to please people but God, who tests our hearts" (1 Thessalonians 2:4). This is the core of being trusted with the signet ring by the King of kings and Lord of lords.

SIGNET RING DECREES

In Jesus' name, I decree that

- *I now receive Your signet ring in order to do Your will on earth and be used by You.*
- *I accept full authority and protection from You to carry out Your eternal purposes on earth.*
- *I have favor with both You and people.*

- *I now operate in zeal for Your glory and appropriate spiritual authority.*
- *I allow myself to be Your vessel in rebuilding the altar as You release Your revival fire on earth to turn people's hearts to You.*

6

A Nation Exiled and Restored

ALEMU BEEFTU

In that day the Lord will snatch away their finery: the bangles and headbands and crescent necklaces, the earrings and bracelets and veils, the headdresses and anklets and sashes, the perfume bottles and charms, the *signet rings* and nose rings, the fine robes and the capes and cloaks, the purses and mirrors, and the linen garments and tiaras and shawls.

Isaiah 3:18–23, emphasis added

Signet rings are a signature that is secured or approved by a higher authority, usually a king, to accomplish what is needed to fulfill his purpose or desire. The authority depends upon the user's character. The king gives his signet ring to authorize a person to carry out a noble purpose for his subjects in his kingdom, like what Pharaoh commissioned Joseph to do for him (see chapter 4). In this chapter, we will look at how the seal of authority was used during the period of the exile of the Jewish people in Babylon, and the period of the Restoration—when they returned to the land of Israel from the nations where they had been scattered. First, the chapter will focus on prophetic voices in the exile—Jeremiah, Ezekiel, Isaiah. Then we will explore the lives of several kings during these two periods in the history of ancient Israel: King Cyrus, King Xerxes and King Darius, whose seal was placed on the lions' den where Daniel was held (see Daniel 6:17). The role of a man named Zerubbabel will also be considered.

Prophetic Voices in the Exile: Jeremiah, Ezekiel, Isaiah

It is interesting that the symbols of the signet ring and signet seals were used by God Himself in speaking to His people in the Old Testament. Let's take a look at some examples.

> Bind up the testimony of warning and seal up God's instruction among my disciples.
>
> Isaiah 8:16

> "As surely as I live," declares the LORD, "even if you, Jehoiachin, son of Jehoiakim king of Judah, were a signet ring on my right hand, I would still pull you off."
>
> Jeremiah 22:24

"Fields will be bought for silver and deeds will be signed, sealed and witnessed in the territory of Benjamin, in the villages around Jerusalem."

Jeremiah 32:44

"Have I not kept this in reserve and sealed it in my vaults?"

Deuteronomy 32:34

Such sealing talks about security, authority and the ownership of God. When God places His seal on something, no one is able to open it without His authority.

A person who opens what has been sealed with the king's signet ring should have not only special permission but also ultimate authority and approval from the king. This picture was well described in Revelation 5. In his revelation, John saw a book or scroll that was sealed in the hand of the One who was seated on the throne. At the same time, he heard an angel asking if there was anybody who was qualified to open the book by breaking the seal. The answer was *no one*. This was not about the ability or power to open the seal, but about the final authority from God to open the seal and read the book.

While the apostle John was weeping, the good news came: "Do not weep! See, the Lion of the tribe of Judah, the Root of David, has triumphed. He is able to open the scroll and its seven seals" (Revelation 5:5). Jesus took the book from the Father, broke the seal and read the scroll. Jesus Christ was the only One, on earth and in the heavens, who had all authority to open what God had closed and sealed. That is why what Jesus Christ shuts, no one can open, and what He opens, no one can shut. In that sense, Jesus Christ was not only given a seal of authority, but He became God's signet ring. Jesus not only opens and closes, but He is the Door. As the final signet ring of God, He is the I AM (see John 8:58).

King Cyrus and the Signet Ring

God had a plan for His covenant people to redeem His treasures for His purposes. God also may give special authority for a special purpose to a person with His approval. King Cyrus was chosen by God to conquer the Babylonians and facilitate the rebuilding of the Temple after seventy years of captivity in Babylon—about 150 years before he was born. He was the king of Persia from 559–530 BC[1] and the last king of the Median kingdom:

> Ambitious and daring, he aligned his kingdom with neighboring peoples and tribes into a solid block of Persian power, then revolted against Astyages of Media. . . . When Cyrus conquered the Median kingdom, however, he came into conflict with Babylon, since the two kingdoms claimed much of the same territory. Cyrus consolidated his power before fighting with Babylon. First, he conquered Asia Minor. Wealthy King Croesus of Lydia and the Lydians submitted to him. Then he overran the northern mountainous region between the Caspian Sea and the northwest corner of India.[2]

Solomon started to build the First Temple in 966 BC. It was destroyed by the Babylonians in 586 BC. Cyrus started to rebuild around 519 BC. The Temple contained the Holy of Holies in Jerusalem. The Holy of Holies was located at the west end of the Temple, and in Solomon's Temple it enshrined the Ark of the Covenant, a symbol of Israel's special relationship with God. The prophet Isaiah described the appointment of King Cyrus:

> "This is what the LORD says to his anointed, to Cyrus, whose right hand I take hold of to subdue nations before him and to strip kings of their armor, to open doors before him so that gates will not be shut: I will go before you and will level the mountains; I will break down gates of bronze and cut through bars of iron. I will give you hidden treasures, riches stored in secret places, so that you may know that I am the LORD, the God of Israel, who summons you by name."
>
> Isaiah 45:1–3

The call and appointment of King Cyrus reflect a type of special assignment. After he came to power, he became extraordinarily strong and brought two kingdoms together under his rule.

The Uniqueness of King Cyrus

Some of the unique facts about King Cyrus, who became the signet ring bearer, include the following:

• Cyrus was not part of the covenant of God. He was not a Jew and didn't know the God of Abraham, Isaac and Jacob. But he was chosen by God before he was born to have the great assignment of releasing God's people and to provide for the rebuilding of the Temple after it was destroyed. The prophecy was told before the Jewish people were taken into captivity. Cyrus would be used by God to conquer the powerful kingdom that

111

would destroy the Temple of God and take the people of covenant captive.

• Cyrus did not have any awareness of the prophecy that the Lord had prepared the way for him to conquer the most powerful kingdom during his time. The Lord dealt with the pride of Babylon by using King Cyrus in accordance with the prophecy of Isaiah: "To Cyrus, whose right hand I take hold of to subdue nations before him and to strip kings of their armor" (Isaiah 45:1). The prophet Habakkuk prophesied a similar thing about the punishment of the Babylonians after God disciplined His people by having the Babylonians deal with them.

• Cyrus became the shepherd of Judah after he conquered the Babylonians, who ruled the Jews with brutality for seventy years, according to Isaiah's prophecy about Cyrus: "He is my shepherd and will accomplish all that I please; he will say of Jerusalem, 'Let it be rebuilt,' and of the temple, 'Let its foundations be laid'" (Isaiah 44:28). He was, therefore, given the seal of approval, God's signet ring, to shepherd God's people, to accomplish God's pleasure, to build the city of God, Jerusalem, and to rebuild the Temple by making a decree and giving support and provision. After he established his kingdom, in the first year of his reign, Cyrus issued a decree permitting the reconstruction of the house of God at Jerusalem to start (see 2 Chronicles 36:22–23; Ezra 1:1–3; 6:2–5) and the return of the Jews, who desired to go back to build the city and rebuild the Temple of God in Jerusalem. The seventy-year period of captivity was prophesied by Jeremiah (see Jeremiah 29:10), and at the end of the seventy years, Daniel prayed for its fulfillment, which ushered King Cyrus into his place (see Daniel 9). When he came into power, he returned sacred vessels taken from the Temple by Nebuchadnezzar seventy years earlier, as well as provided resources for the expenses.

- King Cyrus was anointed by God just like David: "This is what the LORD says to his anointed, to Cyrus" (Isaiah 45:1). The difference was, however, that Cyrus didn't know the Lord at a personal level when the Lord set him apart to be an instrument in rebuilding the city and the Temple of God. The anointing was a sign of God's seal of approval, in accordance with the prophetic words spoken over him before he was born.

Three Key Elements of King Cyrus's Anointing

King Cyrus's anointing was a manifestation of three key elements that every effective leader needs to do the work of God: power, authority and provision. This is a checklist for the transformation of those who have a calling, commitment, character and gifting to correct wrong history and build on the right foundation to shape the future. "Your people will rebuild the ancient ruins and will raise up the age-old foundations; you will be called Repairer of Broken Walls, Restorer of Streets with Dwellings" (Isaiah 58:12). Let us look at the power, authority and provision that comes with this anointing:

- *Power.* When God anointed King Cyrus, He gave him power to do the work Cyrus would not have had the ability or capacity to do in his own strength. We clearly see God's power in Cyrus's ability to subdue nations, strip kings of their armor and open doors (see Isaiah 45:1). Hence, the power of God is the manifested enabling presence of God in an incredibly special and unique way. The seal of the signet ring is when God says, "'Not by might nor by power, but by my Spirit,' says the LORD Almighty" (Zechariah 4:6). That is why the anointing is needed!

- *Authority.* Anointing is not only limited to power, but it also gives authority. Receiving the seal of a king qualifies a person to walk in the authority of that king. Authority is not about ability, but position. Authority is a right to act with legal or official permission. As it is related to anointing, it is walking in divine authority with God. It is what the Lord Himself does for the glory of His name in us, through us and for us. That is what we observe in Cyrus's life. "I will go before you and will level the mountains; I will break down gates of bronze and cut through bars of iron" (Isaiah 45:2). The phrase I will use is *delegated authority.* Walking in authority, therefore, is not trusting in our ability; rather, our trust is in God, and our full obedience is to represent Him. Thus, to have the signet ring is to have full authority to represent His will, desire and pleasure. The base of authority is a relationship that reflects trust, faith and wholehearted obedience.

- *Provision.* Provision is resourcing a person's needs to fulfill their calling. The provision that anointing releases isn't limited to financial resources. God's provision in the lives of called and anointed people includes spiritual gifts, vision, wisdom, favor, resources and a pattern for the work to be done. Moses's experience is a good example. When he was called to bring the people out of Egypt, the first thing he saw was the provision of God's favor. Before that, for forty years Moses was a criminal who should have been killed. Then, when he was sent by God, he was feared and accepted as a leader of God's people because of God's favor. Provision of favor is the most important provision for an effective leader. The second most important provision is guidance. The Lord gave Moses special guidance by His presence, day and night. Furthermore, God made known His ways to Moses; God gave Moses His word, He showed him the pattern for the Tabernacle; He gave him skilled and anointed individuals who could do the work; and finally, He gave Moses abundant financial provision.

When we come to Cyrus, the Lord promised him a hidden treasure that would lead him to know the God of Abraham, Isaac and Jacob. The Lord didn't promise him the rebuilding of the city and the Temple, but gifts for him: "I will give you hidden treasures, riches stored in secret places" (Isaiah 45:3). The amazing thing is that the Lord told him such gifts would lead him into the knowledge of the God of Israel as the Lord and the Creator of everything. The purpose of the provision, therefore, was first to help Cyrus to know who the God of Israel was: "That you may know that I am the LORD, the God of Israel" (Isaiah 45:3). Second, it was to understand his own calling and anointing: "who summons you by name." It was made abundantly clear that the source of all Cyrus's success and accomplishments came from delegated authority, the signet ring, of the Almighty God.

Yes, King Cyrus used his anointing—the seal of approval, the signet ring of the King of Glory—to fulfill his calling by facilitating and providing for God's people to rebuild the city and the Temple of God for greater glory. In the process, the Lord brought Cyrus to the true knowledge of Himself.

King Darius's Officials in the Book of Daniel

During his brief reign as king over the kingdom of the Chaldeans from 538–536 BC, Darius the Mede appointed 120 rulers over the provinces throughout his kingdom, with Daniel and two other administrators over them.[3] These 120 rulers didn't like Daniel because he distinguished himself among them by walking in integrity of character. They decided to trap him. Because he was a faithful worshiper of his God, they knew that he would not compromise in the declaration that for thirty days no one should worship any god but King Darius himself. King Darius sent out the decree in writing and sealed it, in accordance with the law of the Persians and the kingdom of Media.

When Daniel learned about the decree, he went home, opened the upstairs window of his house and started praying three times a day to the God of Abraham, Isaac and Jacob. Daniel refused to worship King Darius. After the rulers saw his dedication to worshiping God, they asked King Darius for permission to throw Daniel into the lions' den. "A stone was brought and placed over the mouth of the den, and the king *sealed* it with his own *signet ring* and with the rings of his nobles so that Daniel's situation might not be changed" (Daniel 6:17, emphasis added).

Sealing the stone with the king's signet ring secured the den from any effort to open it, even by the king himself. But the Lord sealed the lions' mouths, and they were not able to hurt Daniel. The God of Abraham, Isaac and Jacob, the God of true covenant, overturned the enemy's evil plan. Daniel, who trusted God in an exceedingly difficult situation, was rescued by the true and faithful God. Yes, the Lord is able to change the sentence of death for those who trust Him in a life-and-death situation and worship Him in the midst of it.

Zerubbabel as the Lord's Signet Ring

> "On that day," declares the LORD Almighty, "I will take you, my servant Zerubbabel son of Shealtiel," declares the LORD, "and *I will make you like my signet ring*, for I have chosen you," declares the LORD Almighty.
>
> Haggai 2:23, emphasis added

As the grandson of King Jehoiachin of Judah (see 1 Chronicles 3:17–19), Zerubbabel was a descendant of David who was born in Babylon during the exile of the Judeans.[4]

The boy Zerubbabel benefited from his grandfather's favored status, growing up in Babylon's royal court and being educated in politics and military as well as in strong roots of Jewish faith. When Persia overthrew the supposedly-invincible Babylon around 539 B.C., he apparently found new favor from the conquering king, Cyrus II. Under orders from the victorious Persian ruler, Zerubbabel was appointed "governor" over Judah and sent back to Jerusalem in 538 B.C. to lead the effort to rebuild God's Temple there (Ezra 2:1–2; Haggai 1:1).[5]

After King Cyrus II allowed the banished tribe to return to their homeland to rebuild the Temple, he migrated to

Judah.[6] Aside from Revelation 5:5, the most powerful verse using the symbolism of the signet ring is the promise the Lord gave to Zerubbabel through the prophet Haggai: "'I will make you like my signet ring, for I have chosen you,' declares the LORD Almighty" (2:23). A signet ring was given by kings to favored individuals as a sign of promotion to higher authority, so they could handle the king's business in his kingdom with full confidence. The ring was the final approval letter given by a king, and it could not be altered. The uniqueness of this particular verse is that the Lord did not promise to give His signet ring to Zerubbabel. God chose Zerubbabel to *be* His signet ring.

The Lord did not promise to give His signet ring to Zerubbabel. God chose Zerubbabel to be His signet ring.

That means Zerubbabel's life became the Lord's standard of operation and approval. He was united with God's purpose in covenant to reflect who God is and His final authority. In this context, becoming God's signet ring was about being one with God—belonging. It was a true picture of closeness, protection and the care of God. It was a picture of the life of the Lord Jesus Christ and the relationship He had with the Father: "This is my Son, whom I love; with him I am well pleased" (Matthew 17:5). That was the reason Jesus said boldly and publicly, "I and the Father are one" (John 10:30). Furthermore, He declared, "Anyone who has seen me has seen the Father" (John 14:9). You, too, should become the Lord's signet ring by becoming one with God to reflect His glory, to do His will and fulfill His purpose on earth with His full authority and approval.

In the case of Zerubbabel, God honored him at the highest level to use him as a seal of approval of His will and purpose in the rebuilding of the Temple for the greater glory. As a signet ring on the hand of the Lord, he was set apart to establish the standard for God's work. He was carried as a signet ring on the right hand of the God of covenant for his leadership call. It was a sign of God's promise to protect him during the shaking of nations for His purpose. "Zerubbabel is here owned as God's servant, and it is an honorable mention that is hereby made of him, as Moses and David my servants."[7] To fulfill his delegated authority as a signet ring on a finger, he kept close to God, the highest possible honor and glory. Because of his position in the eyes of God, Zerubbabel was given final authority.

The fact that the Lord called Zerubbabel His signet ring gave him approved authority not only to build the house but to inspect it for final approval. Zerubbabel was given the plumb line for the final examination of the work of the Temple. This distinctive standard and God's approval brought great joy to those who had come back from captivity to rebuild the Temple: "These seven [eyes] shall rejoice when they see the plumb line in the hand of Zerubbabel" (Zechariah 4:10 AMP). Zerubbabel was chosen by God both to do the work and to receive the plumb line to establish the standard that would reflect the glory and greatness of God.

Since the Lord chose Zerubbabel to be His signet ring, he would complete the work he started. In the context of his calling as a signet ring, this is a picture of security, protection, provision, power and authority to finish the work of God with great joy. Because of such authority, nothing would stop Zerubbabel from building the Temple, which would host greater glory than the one the enemy had destroyed. In

spite of all the challenges that threatened the rebuilding of
the Lord's Temple, the Lord gave an unchangeable covenant
by making Zerubbabel His own signet ring. That meant God
took the responsibility to make the impossible possible for
him by giving him strength, power and resources that he did
not have: "He said to me, 'This is the word of the Lord to
Zerubbabel: "'Not by might nor by power, but by my Spirit,'
says the Lord Almighty"'" (Zechariah 4:6). When the Lord
said to Zerubbabel "by my Spirit," all the challenges and
threats were settled. Who can stop God? Who can fight with
the Spirit of God? What does God lack?

That doesn't mean that the enemy doesn't fight. In fact,
when enemies of God's people heard about the building of
the Temple, they devised multiple strategies to stop it, using
every weapon they had. But they were not able to overcome
God. The Bible does not promise us that the enemy will not
forge his weapon against us. The promise is that his weapon
will not prevail. "No weapon forged against you will prevail,
and you will refute every tongue that accuses you. This is
the heritage of the servants of the Lord, and this is their
vindication from me" (Isaiah 54:17).

These enemies did not use just one method to stop God's
work. They use various methods: discouraging the people,
making them afraid, hiring counselors to work against them,
frustrating their plans, accusing them falsely, intimidating
them and using force. Yet none of these weapons stopped
God's people from building the Temple. In the midst of the
challenges, the Lord told Zerubbabel the mountain of opposition would be removed by the power of the Holy Spirit. The
Lord Himself spoke to the mountain of opposition and resis-
tance by saying, "What are you, mighty mountain? Before
Zerubbabel you will become level ground" (Zechariah 4:7).

Furthermore, the completion of the Temple by Zerubbabel was declared by God: "The hands of Zerubbabel have laid the foundation of this temple; his hands will also complete it. Then you will know that the LORD Almighty has sent me to you" (v. 9).

Moreover, as a signet ring of the Lord, Zerubbabel was in the presence of God all the time. One of the greatest blessings of being the Lord's signet ring is dwelling in the presence of God. Zerubbabel is a picture of the Messiah. "Christ is the 'signet' on God's hand: always in the Father's presence, ever pleasing in his sight."[8] Zerubbabel was described as one of the anointed ones who give golden oil and stand in the presence of the Lord of the entire earth (see Zechariah 4:14). He is pictured like a green olive tree. That is a sign of not only abiding with God but abiding in Him. Zerubbabel received the Lord's mark on what he did. Wow! His ministry was approved and accepted by God.

King Xerxes in the Book of Esther

King Xerxes was king of the Persian Empire from 485–465 BC, as we read in the book of Esther.[9] After he came into power, King Xerxes organized these types of feasts. During his reign, the Persian Empire was extended from India to Cush, known today as Ethiopia. The territory included 127 provinces. What an ego-booster for King Xerxes to invite the princes, nobles, officials and military leaders of all the Persian and Median kingdoms. He prepared a banquet early in his reign for all his nobles and officials.

As mentioned in chapter 1, one way for kings to express joy was to show off their wealth, power and greatness by creating special events. They looked for opportunities to display their riches, wealth and power to demonstrate their kingdom's strength. These occasions would intimidate their enemies. By displaying their wealth, subjects and territories, they would win faithful allies and loyal servants. The invitation letters were sent with the seal of the king's signet ring to prove that the invitation was genuinely from the king.

King Xerxes, also known as Ahasuerus, demonstrated this extravagant display of power and greatness. As recorded in the book of Esther, King Xerxes, king of the Persian Empire, prepared a special feast for his nobles, officials and military leaders from Persia and the kingdom of Media. The princes were from 127 provinces, from India to Cush, modern-day Ethiopia. King Xerxes was counted as one of the three kings of biblical history who ruled over the entire globe; the other two were Ahab and Nebuchadnezzar. For six months, he displayed his power, wealth, splendor and majesty. "For a full 180 days he displayed the vast wealth of his kingdom and the splendor and glory of his majesty" (Esther 1:4). It is hard to imagine a six-month-long banquet where wealth, splendor and majesty were displayed to show the power of a king.

King Xerxes was so proud that he showed the riches of his glorious kingdom to his princes. This demonstration was especially sinful, as he had all the sacred vessels from the sanctuary taken from his royal treasure-house to the banquet in order to boast of his possessions. This was an offense against God and the Jews. He piled up great treasures and, in his stinginess and greed, hid them. Years later, these are the same treasures that were used to rebuild the Temple.

But even six months was not enough! After that, he prepared another banquet for seven days in a closed garden of his palace. This one was for all the people in Susa, the winter capital. This particular banquet was to show the generosity of King Xerxes. Everything was in abundance. "By the king's command each guest was allowed to drink with no restrictions, for the king instructed all the wine stewards to serve each man what he wished" (v. 8). On the last day of this extravagant banquet, King Xerxes commanded his servants "to bring before him Queen Vashti, wearing her royal crown, in order to display her beauty to the people and nobles, for she was lovely to look at" (v. 11). Queen Vashti had organized her own banquet for women in the king's palace, however. Two banquets were going on at the same time.

When the king's servants delivered the king's message for Queen Vashti to wear her royal crown and join their banquet, she refused to come. In other words, she rejected his authority as her king and husband. In addition, her banquet in the king's palace was in competition with his. The king became very angry. After he sought the advice of his wise men, he made a decree that Queen Vashti would never again enter into the presence of the king. She would be replaced by a better queen, and her royal position would be given to another woman. The decree had his signet ring's seal and was distributed throughout his kingdom. The decree was dispatched "to each province in its own script and to each people in their own language, proclaiming that every man should be ruler over his own household" (v. 22). That is to say, the decree reestablished the authority structure in his home.

This is an immensely powerful picture and object lesson for the Church of Jesus Christ even today. Throughout Church history, similar things have taken place many, many times. Like Queen Vashti, the Church prepares its own feast and organizes a banquet to celebrate its program, while missing what the King of kings Himself has prepared for her. Today, the Body of Christ is too preoccupied by its own activities and, as a result, it rejects the King's invitation to be in His presence. Like Queen Vashti, the Body of Christ has undermined the authority of King Jesus and the headship of Christ. I believe this is the season to reestablish the divine order to exalt the Lord Jesus Christ, the Head and the Bridegroom. For individual churches and denominations who reject the invitation of the King to be in His presence, the time of replacement is not far off. This is not a new concept, but a reminder of what is written in the book of Revelation: "Remember the heights from which you have fallen, and repent . . . and do the works you did at first [when you first knew Me]; otherwise, I will visit you and remove your lampstand . . . from its place" (2:5 AMP).

Like Queen Vashti, the Church prepares its own feast and organizes a banquet to celebrate its program, while missing what the King of kings Himself has prepared for her.

The reason for the warning was that the church in Ephesus had left her first love. That is, she neglected her relationship with the Lord Jesus Christ. The Ephesian church no longer exists today. If there is no repentance and return to the King, the consequence to the Church and believers is the same as for Queen Vashti—being removed and replaced. This is not about eternal security, but about losing the light and becoming ineffective in being the light of the world.

After the king's decree, he appointed officials in every province to gather beautiful young virgins as a replacement for Queen Vashti. Esther was among the beautiful young virgins brought to the palace and placed under the care of

Hegai, the eunuch in charge of Ahasuerus's harem. Mordecai from the tribe of Benjamin lived in Susa and had adopted Esther as a daughter. The virgins were all given special treatment: "Before a young woman's turn came to go in to King Xerxes, she had to complete twelve months of beauty treatments prescribed for the women, six months with oil of myrrh and six with perfumes and cosmetics" (Esther 2:12).

Upon arrival for her treatment, Esther won the favor of everyone who saw her. After she completed her treatment, it was her turn to present herself to King Xerxes. Esther won the heart and favor of King Xerxes and became the queen of the Persian Empire. "Now the king was attracted to Esther more than to any of the other women, and she won his favor and approval more than any of the other virgins. So he set a royal crown on her head and made her queen instead of Vashti" (v. 17).

Esther soon faced the challenge of her life, however. Haman, who had become an immensely powerful leader in the Persian Empire as second only to King Xerxes, wanted everyone to bow down to him. But Mordecai, as a Jew, refused to worship Haman the way he had commanded. This made Haman extremely angry, to the extent that he decided not only to kill Mordecai but to destroy all the Jewish people in the Persian Empire. He convinced the king and also made a financial offer to destroy the Jews. Without understanding his true motive, King Xerxes gave Haman full authority to destroy the Jews when he "took his *signet ring* from his finger and gave it to Haman son of Hammedatha, the Agagite, the enemy of the Jews" (Esther 3:10, emphasis added).

In ancient times, one way to display the king's joy was to show off his wealth, power and greatness by creating occasions to do so. Kings looked for opportunities to demonstrate their riches and power. From time to time, kings sent out sealed invitations to leaders in the kingdom and honored guests for special feasts and celebrations. Those invitations were typically used for two main reasons. The first one was to build relationships and separate loyal servants from others. When a king identified faithful servants, they became closer to him, both to protect him and to do his will. The second reason was to show his power and wealth to intimidate his foes. This type of invitation letter was sent out sealed with a king's signet ring. The seal was to prove that the invitation was from the king and that the invitation was authentic.

As a symbol of the decree, King Xerxes gave his signet ring to Haman (see Esther 3:10). When Haman secured the king's signet ring, he selected the month and dates to write a decree to destroy the Jews. It was sent to governors and officials. "These were written in the name of King Xerxes himself and sealed with his own ring" (v. 12). In every city and country, the Israelites who heard or read the edict were bewildered by this death sentence sealed with the king's signet ring. Great sadness and a cloud of death covered the people because of one person who used the king's signet ring for personal revenge. But the good news was that the Lord's intervention stopped the annihilation of the Israelites, and the edict was reversed. The power of the signet ring representing the covenant between God and His people can never be underestimated. The goodness and promises of God overcome the enemy's evil plans. "Treasures gained by wickedness do not profit" (Proverbs 10:2 ESV).

Haman persuaded King Xerxes by donating ten thousand talents of silver to the royal treasury so he might send out a decree that was sealed with the king's signet ring. The Jewish people were to be destroyed on an appointed day. Mordecai was the one who had uncovered a conspiracy to assassinate the king by two of the king's officers who guarded the doorway. He informed Queen Esther about their plan and saved the king. Mordecai always sat at the gate and watched out for the well-being of his adopted daughter, the queen. Even after she became queen, she listened and obeyed his advice. When Mordecai read the edict against the Jews, he tore his clothes, put on sackcloth and went into the city streets, crying with a loud voice and bitterness of heart. The rest of the Jews joined in a similar wailing, bitter cries and fasting.

When Esther was told about Mordecai's wailing in the city street, she was dumbfounded and became miserable. She sent him new clothes so that he could take off the sackcloth. But he refused to accept the clothes the queen sent. Finally, she sent one of her attendants to find out what was happening to Mordecai. He told the attendant the full story regarding the edict that ensured a massacre of all the Jews in the Persian Empire. But Mordecai saw an opportunity. He sent the attendant back, asking that Queen Esther go to King Xerxes and intercede for her people. Queen Esther replied that she could not approach the king without his invitation. If she were to go in to plead for her people without being summoned, she would be killed. After he received her response, Mordecai sent her a stronger message. "If you remain silent at this time, relief and deliverance for the Jews will arise from another place, but you and your father's family will perish. And who knows but that you have come to your royal position for such a time as this?" (Esther 4:14).

Upon receiving this strong message from her uncle, Esther asked him to organize three days of fasting and prayer.

"When this is done, I will go to the king, even though it is against the law. And if I perish, I perish" (v. 16). After the three days of fasting and prayer, Esther dressed in her royal robes and entered the inner court of the palace, in front of the king's throne. The three days of fasting and prayer had prepared the king's heart. When he saw Queen Esther, he was pleased and extended the gold scepter to her, according to the custom. By touching the tip of the king's scepter, she not only secured her safety, but she received the greatest possible favor from the king to ask for anything she desired. That was why he said to her, "What is it, Queen Esther? What is your request? Even up to half the kingdom, it will be given you" (5:3).

Esther knew the need was not half of King Xerxes's kingdom, but, instead, authority to reverse the death sentence decreed over her people. The Lord blessed Esther not only with beauty, great favor and determination, but also with a divine strategy to save her nation. She answered the king's question by inviting him, along with Haman, to a feast she would prepare. The king accepted Queen Esther's invitation with great delight and told his servant to get Haman at once to go to the dinner Esther had prepared. "As they were drinking wine, the king again asked Esther, 'Now what is your petition? It will be given you. And what is your request? Even up to half the kingdom, it will be granted'" (v. 6).

The Lord blessed Esther not only with beauty, great favor and determination, but also with a divine strategy to save her nation.

Queen Esther, filled with wisdom, invited the king and Haman for a second dinner party. In spite of the situation's urgency, she decided to wait for the right timing. The king accepted the invitation and went to his palace for a night of rest. But two key things took place that night. Haman was excited because Queen Esther had honored him by inviting him along with the king to dinner. Haman saw Mordecai again, who refused to bow down before him. This drove Haman mad. When he told his friends and wife, they advised him to have a massive set of gallows built. He should speak with the king in the morning and hang Mordecai on them, then happily go to the dinner. He took their advice, built the gallows and went to speak with the king in the early morning.

The king, who went back to his palace after the feast, was not able to sleep. He asked his servant to read to him from the record book—the journal of events in his kingdom. While reading, they came across the history that Mordecai had uncovered and exposed the plot of two royal guards who had conspired to assassinate King Xerxes. The king's immediate question was, "What honor and recognition has Mordecai received for this?" The answer was none. When the king asked, "Who is in the king's court?" It just happened that Haman was in the court. He had come early to speak to the king about hanging Mordecai on the gallows that he had built overnight. The king asked Haman, "What should be done for the man the king delights to honor?" (Esther 6:6). Haman thought the king was talking about honoring him. So, without hesitation, he listed all the things that should be done for the man the king wished to honor. "Let them robe the man the king delights to honor, and lead him on the horse through the city streets, proclaiming before him, 'This is what is done for the man the king delights to honor!'" (v. 9). After he finished, the king told him to go and do the very thing he had described for Mordecai. And so Haman did that very thing for Mordecai all day long.

At the feast that evening, after Haman had been forced to honor the man he hated, Esther entreated the king. She told King Xerxes that her people were about to be massacred and eliminated altogether. Outraged, the king asked who had perpetrated such a thing. Queen Esther answered the king by saying, "An adversary and enemy! This vile Haman!" (7:6). That night, the king acted on Esther's behalf, and Haman was hanged on the gallows he had built for Mordecai.

After the hanging, "Mordecai came into the presence of the king, for Esther had told how he was related to her. *The king took off his signet ring*, which he had reclaimed from Haman, *and presented it to Mordecai*" (8:1–2, emphasis added). The king asked Mordecai and Esther to write another proclamation in his name on behalf of the Jews and seal it with the king's signet ring. The instructions would be sent out throughout the Persian Empire. Mordecai took advantage of the opportunity and wrote a new decree, which overturned what Haman had written for the destruction of the Jewish people, and sealed it with the king's signet ring. It was then sent to 127 countries throughout the empire with the fastest of the royal horses.

This decree gave the Jewish people the right and authority to arm and defend themselves from the threat of their enemies. Furthermore, Mordecai was promoted. He received a royal robe, gold crown and purple cape of fine linen. "On the thirteenth day of the twelfth month," the decree was written and sealed by the king's signet ring—the day the Jews' enemies had hoped to overpower and destroy them (9:1). But because of Esther's determination and Mordecai's faithfulness, the tables were turned. The Jews overpowered their enemies and made it a day of joy and celebration rather than destruction. With appropriate usage, the king's signet ring saved the nation!

Mordecai demonstrated the power of servanthood. Although the Jews were enslaved and ruled by King Xerxes and his kingdom, their dedication to God's covenant gave them the power to rise above their slavery. The influence of Mordecai and Esther became more powerful than the Persian laws. God's covenant is stronger than the king's covenant and his signet ring.

The authority of God is available to each of us, no matter our circumstances. According to Esther, chapter 2, Esther, the niece of Mordecai, was adopted by him because her mother and father had died. Her uncle did what was right in the eyes of God. Because Mordecai was a righteous man, he had God-given authority. He, in turn, instructed Esther what she should do to gain the favor of King Xerxes. We can conclude that we, too, are able to redeem our heavenly treasures when we do what is right in the eyes of God. In a time of turmoil all around us, God is able to give us His eternal plan for our lives.

Do you have the authority and security, through God's anointing, in your life to release His power, authority and provision to accomplish His will? His pleasure is for us to know Him, honor Him, worship Him and use our spiritual power and authority to facilitate others to build His Temple. We are accountable to the Giver and Provider at the end of our lives. Let us use the signet ring with responsibility and a greater desire to know Him.

———— SIGNET RING DECREES ————

In Jesus' name, I decree that

- *You have given me not only secial permission but also ultimate authority and approval.*
- *Your people will rebuild the ancient ruins and will raise up the age-old foundations.*
- *Your people will be called Repairer of Broken Walls, Restorer of Streets with Dwellings.*
- *I will worship You, even in the midst of life-and-death situations.*
- *I now receive security, protection, provision, power and authority to finish the work You started in me.*

PART III

SIGNET RINGS IN
the New Covenant

7

Restoration of the Signet Ring

Alemu Beeftu

"Do not work for food that spoils, but for food that endures to eternal life, which the Son of Man will give you. For on him God the Father has placed his seal of approval."

John 6:27

In part II, we looked at the signet ring in ancient Israel. Now we turn our attention to the signet ring in the New Covenant. As we have discussed, the signet ring carries a significant level of authority, security, honor, ownership, covenant relationship, family identity and signature, as well as delegated power to accomplish a given assignment. The goal of this chapter is to show the link between the first man

135

(Adam) and the second Adam (Jesus), then discuss Jesus as the signet ring of the Father and our High Priest. Lastly, the chapter will highlight the sources of Jesus' authority: His Sonship, submission and service, the Spirit of God and sacrifice.

The First Man and the Signet Ring

In the case of Adam, he was given a seal of approval to rule and manage the earth. God's supreme desire and purpose for creating the human race was to have relationships with others to interact with and trust with delegated authority, as faithful ambassadors. Our Father wanted sons and daughters with whom He could partner in His heavenly kingdom enterprise. Earth was the Father's gift to His newly created sons and daughters.

In the Genesis account of creation, we see that God chose to create humankind (male and female) on day six, the final day before He rested. Six is a number in Scripture that often symbolizes man. Isn't it interesting that six plus six equals twelve, the number indicative of governmental perfection? Twelve is the number, or factor of all numbers, connected with government—whether by tribes or apostles, in the measurement of time or in other things that have to do with government in the heavens and on earth. It applies to divine and apostolic government.

Humankind was created for the overarching purpose of ruling and reigning with God on earth. God's ultimate purpose for humankind was, and still is, to colonize earth and cause it to look and operate just like heaven. In cooperation with God, Adam and Eve were to manage the planet. He made us like Himself originally, with all the authority necessary to dominate the earth, nature and the rest of creation. This position of authority, by the way, does not include domination over fellow human beings. Humankind is called and given authority by God's signet ring, or seal. That is God's creation mandate for humankind (see Genesis 1:26–28). Humans were created in God's image, so we are able to rule the earth with and for Him. As a sign of full authority, God put His seal on Adam when He breathed into him the breath of life (see Genesis 2:7).

God created Adam and then breathed into him the breath of life. Adam bore the image and likeness of God and possessed within himself the life-giving Spirit of the Almighty. Humans were designed to be a type of Holy Spirit container. This foundational element of our existence, God's Spirit residing within us, is what qualified Adam for his relationship with God and gave him the authority to rule the earth. Being in relationship with His created beings is God's priority, and it must be ours, as well, if we are to use His signet ring for His glory and become a signet ring ourselves.

At creation, God brought Adam forth from the unseen realm of heaven—God's abode—into the seen, visible realm we know as earth. In His forethought and wisdom, God placed Adam in the environment designed and created for him: Eden, the place of God's presence. God's design was for Eden to serve as Adam's training ground. Adam was in training to be used as God's signet ring through intimate relationship with his Creator. Eden was God's chosen place on earth, designed for His first son, Adam, the place of uninhibited, unrestricted relational experience while becoming the signet ring of God. Adam used God's signet ring the first time when he named animals. "Whatever the man called each living creature, that was its name" (v. 19). The name was the seal of approval.

We know the story all too well. Adam sinned and fell from his rightful position with God and, as a result, stepped out of his place of protection and blessing by misusing the authority, honor and power given him by God. As a result of his choice, Adam removed himself from his course of purpose promised by God. He chose to cut himself off from right alignment and spiritual authority to rule the earth for the glory of God.

God always has been, and always will be, concerned about man's proper position in relation to Himself while walking in authority to fulfill His purpose on earth. In this regard, His eternal plan for humankind has not changed. It is still His ultimate desire for us to be right with Him relationally, spiritually and in every other sense. In order to complete what we were destined for, we must be correctly positioned and aligned with the King of the universe to be trusted with His signet ring. The degree to which we are rightly aligned with God and His will for our lives will determine the level of our authority with which we are able to fulfill His destiny and assignment on earth.

The degree to which we are rightly aligned with God and His will for our lives will determine the level of our authority with which we are able to fulfill His destiny and assignment on earth.

Adam's assignment was simply a matter of carrying out God's divine agenda by exercising the power that was given him to rule the earth for the glory of God. Adam was to glorify his Creator by becoming like Him and doing His will. You are familiar with this assignment as given in Ephesians 2:10: "We are God's handiwork, created in Christ Jesus to do good works, which God prepared in advance for us to do." Humankind was

God's crowning accomplishment, and after it, He rested. The idea that God rested implies that following this rest, God ceased His creative efforts. Humans are God's highest and last achievement in the order of creation. Upon further study of the meaning of God's resting on the seventh day, we find this was a day of celebration and rejoicing over the work of His own hands. Our Creator celebrated His creation— humankind—whom He had made to be the mirror image of Himself; one like Him, who could be trusted with the signet ring of the Lord. We were made to carry the glory of our Creator. We have been designed and destined to manifest His beautiful, powerful nature in earth's realm. We live to exhibit the qualities of the eternal King of the universe. We become a blessing to our God and others by discovering and fulfilling the purpose of our existence—His seal of approval!

Such was the anticipatory heart of our Father, who gave charge of His business, the family business—planet earth—to His offspring. He created the earth for humankind and placed it in our care. His signet ring was given to humankind to manage His business. The process of "becoming," therefore, is one aspect of accepting our God-given responsibility. Adam neglected the priority of staying in right relationship, which was essential to accomplish his assignment. Becoming who we are in relation to God positions us to receive authority and power to carry out His will.

The Last Adam and the Signet Ring

The fall of man resulted in separation from God. Jesus' mission in coming to earth was to restore us to the place of perfect fellowship with our Father. As I have mentioned, becoming who we are meant to be requires a process—a journey of going back to a right relationship with our heavenly Father by becoming His children. The last Adam came to bring us back to where we can have the signet ring of the King through relationship. That is why when a person accepts the Lord Jesus Christ, they are given authority to become a child of God. That is receiving the signet ring as a family identity.

Let's examine the difference between the leadership of the first Adam and that of the last Adam (see 1 Corinthians 15:45). The first Adam was in the Garden of Eden. What happened to him? He didn't submit to anyone. He rejected the authority of God. God the Father directed the last Adam, Jesus Christ, like a child. And Jesus willingly went through the process. He did not learn obedience through popularity. He learned it through suffering. "Even though Jesus was God's Son, he learned obedience from the things he suffered" (Hebrews 5:8 NLT). Suffering builds character. God allowed His Son to suffer so He would learn obedience. With obedience, God gave Jesus the authority to fulfill His purpose.

When the first Adam left his place of fellowship with God, several things occurred.

- Humankind's relationship with God was broken.
- Humankind's relationship between each other was broken.
- Humankind's glory was replaced by shame.
- A false sense of responsibility was assumed to cover humankind's shame and guilt.
- The Garden and assignment of God for humankind became their place of hiding.
- Humankind ran *away* from God instead of *to* Him.

- Blessing was replaced by a curse.
- A generation would be neglected—as an example, Adam and Eve did not know when Cain killed Abel.

The second Adam, the Lord Jesus Christ, came to pay the price to restore us to God's image, give us God's life and reestablish our relationship with God so that we could be trusted with the King's signet ring. He made us a new creation and elevated our position with Him: "God raised us up with Christ and seated us with Him in the heavenly realms in Christ Jesus" (Ephesians 2:6 BSB). The Lord Jesus gave us the highest power and authority in His Kingdom, thereby sharing His throne with us and seating us with Himself. The highest authority any king can give is to share his throne. What an authority and responsibility!

When a person is out of alignment relationally, his "ministry" or "business" becomes the end itself rather than a means to accomplish God's will. This is idolatry. Whatever we prize or value more highly than God Himself becomes an idol in our lives. We know without a doubt that God will not tolerate idolatry in any form, even when we think we are secure just because we were trusted with authority in the past. That is why the Lord said to Jehoiachin, king of Judah, "'As surely as I live,' declares the LORD, 'even if you, Jehoiachin, son of Jehoiakim king of Judah, were a signet ring on my right hand, I would still pull you off'" (Jeremiah 22:24). This Scripture is a powerful mental image for us today.

The key to operating in integrity of character is a right personal relationship and communion with God. Character formation is a process. It is the journey of becoming like Him. The source of spiritual authority is a genuine and sincere relationship with God. The process of becoming who we were created to be prepares us for our destiny and divine destination, allowing us to walk with divine authority. When we are rightly aligned with God, He will reveal Himself and trust us with His signet ring to represent Him on earth.

That is why the Lord Jesus Christ came to restore our relationship with our Father by removing our sin and iniquity through His blood. "To him who loves us and has freed us from our sins by his blood, and has made us to be a kingdom and priests to serve his God and Father—to him be glory and power for ever and ever! Amen" (Revelation 1:5–6). Proper alignment with God positions us to receive from Him everything that is needed on this side of heaven to advance His Kingdom agenda. As New Testament believers, the idea of creation and formation has everything to do with what is accomplished within our spirit man at the time of the new birth. When we are reborn spiritually, we are re-created in the likeness of Christ, the One who created humans initially. It is at this point in time when the reformation process begins.

As a result of the new birth, humans are qualified to fulfill the will and purposes of God, and once again they become ambassadors of heaven assigned to earth. When we align ourselves with God and come into right relationship with Him through faith in Christ, we receive everything necessary to birth His purposes and bear fruit on earth, since we are the seal of the Holy Spirit: "When you heard the word of truth, the good news of your salvation, and [as a result] believed in Him, were stamped with the seal of the promised Holy Spirit [the One promised by Christ] as owned and protected [by God]" (Ephesians 1:13 AMP). The Lord made us a new creation with that sealing of the Holy Spirit. That means the signet ring that was taken from Adam is now given to us by the Lord Jesus, the second Adam. He restored to us the authority to be fruitful again. Adam and Eve lost their authority because of sin.

Through spiritual restoration, the Lord Jesus restored us to the place where we carry and reflect the image of God. God created us to reflect His glory—the manifest essence of His nature. Because we are so like Him, we are capable of reflecting Him. Once we are in our right place in Him, we will be like mirrors as He shines on us, in us and through us. This glorification of God happens only as we possess His character. As we become like Him in this respect, we become His expression on earth. That is becoming His signet ring. It is only through relationship with God that we are gloriously changed into the image of His Son to represent Him on earth.

Vital union with the King is the foundation for who we are and what we are doing. When we are in right relationship with Him, everything He has given us can be used as a means to fellowship with Him. Every responsibility He entrusts to our care, big or small, provides a platform from which we can offer Him the worship He desires and deserves. With the Holy Spirit as God's signet ring of authority, we are to follow the command of Jesus. "He said to his disciples, 'The harvest is plentiful but the workers are few. Ask the Lord of the harvest, therefore, to send out workers into his harvest field'" (Matthew 9:37–38).

Jesus as the Signet Ring of the Father

"For on him God the Father has placed his seal of approval."

John 6:27

143

The greatest approval, authority, honor and sign of oneness was given to the Lord Jesus Christ by God our Father, both in the heavens and on earth. The sign of the signet ring was given to the Lord Jesus Christ, the coming Savior of the world, even before the foundation of earth. So when the Word became flesh, He came carrying the seal of approval and authority as the sent One of our Father with full authority and power to be our Savior and Lord. "God the Father has authorized Him and put His seal on Him" (John 6:27 AMP). This Scripture describes everything the Lord Jesus accomplished on earth as our signet ring, as guaranteed by God our Father.

Since Jesus was sent with our Father's approval and authority—as His signet ring—everything is subject to His Lordship.

Since Jesus was sent with our Father's approval and authority—as His signet ring—everything is subject to His Lordship. The Father gave His scepter of authority to rule His enemies and to save those who trust in Him or have come to take refuge under His wing. This authority was promised to Him prophetically long before He became flesh and dwelt with us.

Jesus, Our High Priest

"The LORD has sworn and will not change his mind. 'You are a priest forever, in the order of Melchizedek. The Lord is at your right hand; he will crush kings on the day of his wrath'" (Psalm 110:4–5). That promise was realized fully in the Lord Jesus Christ. The High Priest office was always a picture of Christ, our Savior, who was to come as a perfect high priest, as it was written: "You are a priest forever, in the order of Melchizedek" (Hebrews 5:6).

The order of Melchizedek acknowledges that He is forever with kingly and priestly authority. In describing His authority, the apostle Peter stated the following: "How God anointed Jesus of Nazareth with the Holy Spirit and power, and how he went around doing good and healing all who were under the power of the devil, because God was with him" (Acts 10:38). Hence, anointing is a seal of authority. This is the reason why the Lord Jesus declared He was anointed and sent by the Holy Spirit to fulfill His earthly calling. He started with authority and approval from the Father. At the end of His priestly duty on earth, God the Father gave Him the name above every name and all authority both in the heavens and on earth.

To fulfill God's purpose and will, He told the disciples after the resurrection that He would send them as the Father sent Him. With this power and authority, all who trust in the name of Jesus are set apart by Him to be His ambassadors in His Kingdom until He comes back. That means each believer who has been washed by the blood of Jesus Christ has received this signet ring in the form of the sealing, filling, leading, empowering and anointing of the Holy Spirit. The apostles made this truth clear in the New Testament writings.

The apostle John wrote, "To him who loves us and has freed us from our sins by his blood, and has made us to be *a kingdom and priests* to serve his God and Father—to him be glory and power for ever and ever! Amen" (Revelation 1:5–6, emphasis added). Becoming a king in His Kingdom is to receive the signet ring to serve the King of kings. That is walking with full authority and approval of the King in His Kingdom on earth. We can only exercise the kingly authority if we live the lifestyle of a priest. The call of a priest was described plainly during the Restoration in Israel by King Hezekiah. In calling back the priests to their role, King Hezekiah said to them, "My sons, do not be negligent now, for the LORD has chosen you to stand before him and serve him, to minister before him and to burn incense" (2 Chronicles 29:11). The call of a priest is to stand before God, do His will, worship Him (minister to Him) and bring sacrifices of praise and adoration to the King of Glory.

Kingdom authority is the result of relationship. The King of Glory trusts with His signet ring those who know Him and honor Him daily. The basis for the signet ring is covenant relationship and fellowship with Him: "God's solid foundation stands firm, sealed with this inscription: 'The Lord knows those who are his'" (2 Timothy 2:19). The seal of God on us is to live as His ambassadors with the message of reconciliation: "We are therefore Christ's ambassadors, as though God were making his appeal through us" (2 Corinthians 5:20).

As previously discussed in this chapter, the Lord Jesus came to the world as the second Adam, as the sent One to represent our Father as His signet ring. And Jesus, as our High Priest, always intercedes for us.

The Father's Words in Matthew 17

When God talked about Zerubbabel, He referred to him as His signet ring who was chosen to be His servant. But when He described the Lord Jesus Christ, He said, "This is my Son, whom I love; with him I am well pleased. Listen to him!" (Matthew 17:5). When we look at this verse closely, in the context of a signet ring, these phrases make the Lord Jesus appear above and beyond all others who were trusted with divine authority to represent Him.

- *"This is my son."* The first declaration in Matthew 17:5 is "This is my son." Jesus was not a chosen servant, like Zerubbabel or other faithful servants who were chosen to do His will and purpose. Jesus is the Son of God. That means even though the Word became flesh and dwelt with us as one hundred percent man, at the same time He is one hundred percent God, truly revealing our Father in every aspect of life. The apostle John wrote, "No one has ever seen God, but the one and only Son, who is Himself God and is at the Father's side, has made him known" (John 1:18 BSB). The Lord Jesus carried the signet ring of the Father, therefore, as His Son to reveal the complete attributes of God: His holiness, power, authority, glory, majesty, love, care and compassion.

- *"Whom I love."* Following, is the descriptive phrase "whom I love." Jesus is not only a begotten Son but also a loved Son. He carried the seal of the love of our Father in what He demonstrated among us on earth. "As the Father has loved me, so have I loved you" (John 15:9). One of the things that made Jesus a signet ring of God is the fact that He revealed the Father's heart. Jesus had the same DNA as our heavenly Father.

- *"With him I am well pleased."* The closing declaration in Matthew 17:5 is "With him I am well pleased." It is one thing to be trusted with the King's signet ring, but it is amazing to hear public testimony that the King is well pleased. Whenever ancient kings were pleased with their chosen servants, the kings would increase the level of their authority. The apostle John testified about Jesus' level of authority at the end of His earthly ministry when he wrote, "Jesus knew that the Father had put all things under his power" (John 13:3). Recorded in Scripture by witnesses, Jesus repeated the same after His resurrection before He went back to the Father: "All authority in heaven and on earth has been given to me" (Matthew 28:18).

- *"Listen to him!"* The final instruction in Matthew 17:5 is "Listen to him!" By this, God our Father announced that Jesus Christ was given all authority and power to represent His will and purpose. Paying attention to obey His will is not a matter of opinion or option. This is a command God gave concerning His Son, His signet ring. During His public ministry, the Lord Jesus operated fully in the delegated authority He received. Because of this authority, He was different from other teachers of the law. Even common people recognized and testified to the power of His words and the authority of His life and teaching. "The people were all so amazed that they asked each other, 'What is this? A new teaching—and with authority!'" (Mark 1:27). The authority of His teaching also brought about a demonstration of power. He gave orders to evil spirits, and they obeyed His word without question.

Jesus' word carried healing power along with authority. That is why the centurion said to the Lord, "Just say the word, and my servant will be healed" (Matthew 8:8). Indeed, his servant was healed quickly by the word of the Lord Jesus. The mighty winds and storm became calm at His word. He also raised the dead by the power of His word: "Jesus called in a loud voice, 'Lazarus, come out!' The dead man came out, his hands and feet wrapped with strips of linen, and a cloth around his face" (John 11:43–44). What authority!

Furthermore, Christ's word creates. It brings into existence that which is not there or could not be otherwise. All things are made and sustained by the power of His word. The foundation of everything that can stand and remain forever is His word. In other words, His word provides a strong and lasting foundation for those who would like to build what will last. Those who hear His word and obey will stand on a strong, unshakable foundation. The Lord honors and confirms His word by working with those who declare His word. "The Lord worked with them and confirmed his word by the signs that accompanied it" (Mark 16:20). The apostle Paul testified to very same thing in his ministry: "I will not venture to speak of anything except what Christ has accomplished through me in leading the Gentiles to obey God by what I have said and done—by the power of signs and wonders, through the power of the Spirit" (Romans 15:18–19).

Jesus' Unique Characteristics

Many special characteristics made the Lord Jesus Christ different from all others who were chosen by God to become His signet ring and do His will on earth. To reiterate and add to what was stated above:

- He is the Son of God, one with the Father and sent by our Father. "You are the Christ, the Son of the living God" (Matthew 16:16 NKJV).
- He carries the fullness of God. "It pleased the Father for all the fullness [of deity—the sum total of His essence, all His perfection, powers, and attributes] to dwell [permanently] in Him (the Son)" (Colossians 1:19 AMP).

149

- He was in the Father. "Don't you believe that I am in the Father, and that the Father is in me?" (John 14:10).

- He only spoke the word of the Father in its purity. "The words I say to you I do not speak on my own authority. Rather, it is the Father, living in me, who is doing his work" (John 14:10).

- He lived by and for the will of God like no other person on earth. He is the only One who could say, "My food is to do the will of Him who sent Me and to completely finish His work" (John 4:34 AMP).

God our Father fully trusted Jesus with His perfect will. The Lord Jesus established the true standard of being the signet ring of God through the following sources of authority:

Sources of Jesus' Authority

When we look closely at Jesus' life and ministry and the source of His authority, we see a number of things that gave Him divine authority to be the best and the most effective leader the world has ever known.

1. Sonship

> Yet to all who received him, to those who believed in his name, he gave the right to become children of God.
>
> John 1:12 NIV1984

The foundation of His spiritual authority was *sonship*. Jesus received His authority from God by being His Son. That's how all leaders should establish their authority. Divine authority draws us to God, not away from Him. In essence, Jesus said, *If you want to know My authority, it comes from being the Son of the living God. I submit to My Father. I am the Son of the living God. That's the name I want to take upon Myself. That's where My authority is from.*

The way to establish authority is to become a child of God.

Being a child of the King places us at the highest position of authority. Angels don't have this authority. Angels have authority, but they don't have the same authority we do as children of God. We can get up in the morning and say, "Daddy." Angels cannot call God "Daddy," but Christians can. The greatest authority, the divine authority, therefore, draws us to God.

When you have authority in a ministry, and it begins to draw you away from God, something dangerous is taking place. True authority from God draws us near to Him. When you get up in the morning, what fills your mind? Being a child of God, or a leader? When a leader forgets he or she is a child of God, ministry focus is lost. When you get up and say, "This is my position and this is who I am," you've lost your focus. That's why being a child of God must be the foundation of everything we do.

The biggest problem for most leaders today is that they don't know how to be a child, yet they strive to be effective leaders. If you don't know how to be a child of God, you don't know how to be an effective leader in the Kingdom. If you don't know how to enjoy your Father, you don't know how to receive responsibility from your Father. After all, this is *His* Kingdom. Jesus said, "The disciples were Yours, but they have been given to Me, and I protected them by Your name" (see John 17:12). What name? It was the name of the

Father, and Jesus protected them by the name of His Father. Now He was giving them back to the Father, except the one, Judas, who departed from the group.

Recently, I was on my face praying when my daughter came and lay down on my back. I told her to go back to bed, but she said, "No, Daddy, I want to be with you." *No, Daddy, I want to be with you.* When have you said to the Father, "Daddy, I want to be with You? I just came to be with You." If we forget how to be like a child, we will soon forget how to lead according to the purposes of God. Leadership, biblically defined, does not depend on the mind, it depends on the heart. And a warm heart comes from a relationship with the living God.

The foundation of earthly responsibility is in the understanding that we are in God. Our positions in an organizational structure should not define us. Our relationship with the Almighty One is the foundation of our identity.

Once more: *We establish authority by being children of God.* For a leader, the basis of earthly responsibility is understanding, accepting and operating as a child of the living God. Such a process involves actively learning how to live like a child of God. This includes understanding the importance of relationship. We cannot fulfill our call and purpose in God by isolating ourselves from Him. A divine relationship is the only way to fulfill our calling. That's why Jesus grew both in body and in wisdom, *gaining favor with God and men.* Favor with God results from a relationship with Him and acknowledging Him as the Source of our authority. Favor with people results from recognition of our leadership position.

In Luke 7:30, the Pharisees rejected sonship: "But the Pharisees and the experts in the law rejected God's purpose for themselves, because they had not been baptized by John."

As a result, they never knew true spiritual authority. Sonship enables a leader to know both the power of God and the heart of God. That's why Jesus called the disciples *children* rather than *servants*.

2. Submission and Service

The second source of authority is submission. Submission is a by-product of being a child. Leaders who yield to, submit to and obey God as Father know how to gain spiritual authority to fulfill His calling. But what do *yielding* and *willingness to obey* really mean?

The responsibility of a leader is to fulfill destiny: the leader's personal destiny and the destinies of others. How does one carry this out? It can be done only by submitting to a higher authority. Jesus knew the Pharisees wanted to know the source of His authority. Since He was a child of God, He submitted to the will of His Father and to His purposes. Submission is a true source of authority.

Consider the following example of Jesus' obedience to His Father in heaven.

> Jesus came from Galilee to the Jordan to be baptized by John. But John tried to deter him, saying, "I need to be baptized by you, and do you come to me?"
>
> Jesus replied, "Let it be so now; it is proper for us to do this to fulfill all righteousness." Then John consented.
>
> As soon as Jesus was baptized, he went up out of the water. At that moment heaven was opened, and he saw the Spirit of God descending like a dove and alighting on him. And a voice from heaven said, "This is my Son, whom I love; with him I am well pleased."
>
> Matthew 3:13–17

Jesus went to the Jordan River. Why? He didn't go because He wanted to submit to John. John, who was less than He, had come to prepare the way for Him. Yet Jesus willingly submitted to John in baptism. Authority comes through submission. Jesus went to the River Jordan to ask John to baptize Him, but John said it was he whom Jesus should baptize. Jesus said it must be this way in order to fulfill all righteousness. Because Jesus submitted to John, He received authority.

3. The Spirit of God

Jesus' commissioning came *after* the descent of the Holy Spirit. The Father said, "This is my Son, whom I love; with him I am well pleased." God is not pleased with who we are, nor is He impressed with what we do for Him. We can't impress God. He was pleased with His beloved Son, because He was willing to submit to John, the man who came to prepare the way for Him. In so doing, Jesus demonstrated humility. He died to self. The Father said, "With him I am well pleased"(Matthew 3:17).

The source of power and authority both in the Old Testament and the New Testament is God. The Holy Spirit gives true spiritual authority. There is no leadership office without spiritual authority. In the Old Testament, priests, kings and prophets were anointed to function with authority in their offices. In the New Testament, the Lord Jesus gave authority to those He called and appointed to do the work of the Kingdom. The Holy Spirit came upon those who were called and set apart to give them power and authority to do the work of God as leaders.

According to the Bible, the Holy Spirit came upon many leaders to confirm their calling by giving them power and authority to assume their leadership roles. For instance, in the Old Testament we see this happen to Joshua (see Deuteronomy 34:9), Gideon (see Judges 6:34), Samson (see Judges 13:25; 14:6), Saul (see 1 Samuel 10:6, 10), David (see 1 Samuel 16:13), and Elisha (see 2 Kings 2:15), among others.

We see similar workings of God in the New Testament. Even the Lord Jesus carried out the will of His Father with the spiritual authority that the Holy Spirit gave Him. Before He stepped into His role at His baptism, the Holy Spirit came upon Him (see Matthew 3:16). In the gospel of John, we are told that the Holy Spirit remained upon Him (see John 1:33). As a result, Jesus Himself said He was given authority (see Matthew 8:9). He taught with authority (see Matthew 7:29). He healed with authority (see Matthew 9:8). He preached the good news with authority (see Luke 4:18). He cleansed the Temple with authority (see Matthew 21:23).

The same thing happened to the apostles. After the resurrection, the Lord Jesus breathed into the apostles, and they received the Holy Spirit. He also told them to stay in Jerusalem until they received the power to fulfill their calling. According to the promise, they received power and authority from the Holy Spirit on the day of Pentecost (see Acts 2).

4. Sacrifice

> The next day John saw Jesus coming toward him and said, "Look, the Lamb of God, who takes away the sin of the world!"
>
> John 1:29

The willingness to be used by God is the basis of spiritual authority. Jesus was fully committed to being used by His Father. He gave His life to become the sacrificial lamb.

Isaiah saw this role for the Messiah long ago and wrote Isaiah 53 in response to his God-given insight. Jesus came to fulfill that prophecy in Isaiah by dying on the cross and shedding His blood for the remission of sin. That is why He said, "Sacrifice and offering you did not desire, but a body you prepared for me; with burnt offerings and sin offerings you were not pleased. Then I said, 'Here I am—it is written about me in the scroll—I have come to do your will, my God'" (Hebrews 10:5–9).

Jesus went to the cross in obedience, to be sacrificed for our sins by emptying Himself of His glory (see Philippians 2). "Christ, our Passover lamb, has been sacrificed" (1 Corinthians 5:7). Jesus died, was buried and rose on the third day. After He paid the price, God the Father gave Him the name that is above every name (see Philippians 2:9–11). Because of the price He paid: "Jesus came to them and said, 'All authority in heaven and on earth has been given to me'" (Matthew 28:18).

As a leader, to whom are you accountable to for your spiritual walk? Do you have a John in your life? Leaders who die to self and pride are acting out of submission and have true authority. When Jesus submitted to authority, not only did heaven open, but also the power of the Holy Spirit came upon Him. Our spiritual authority to impact the Kingdom is equivalent to our anointing. Anointing can increase, but it depends on our daily relationship with the Lord. We can increase or decrease our anointing.

—— SIGNET RING DECREES ——

In Jesus' name, I decree that

- *You came to pay the price to restore me to Your image.*
- *You are reestablishing my relationship with You so I can be trusted with Your signet ring.*
- *You have given me divine authority to represent You.*
- *I am becoming who You created me to be.*
- *I now walk with divine authority.*
- *I will arrive at my divine destination in Your timing.*

8

The Signet Ring
and Sonship

ALEMU BEEFTU

"The father said to his servants, 'Quickly bring out the best robe [for the guest of honor] and put it on him; and give him a ring for his hand, and sandals for his feet. And bring the fattened calf and slaughter it, and let us [invite everyone and] feast and celebrate; for this son of mine was [as good as] dead and is alive again; he was lost and has been found.'"

Luke 15:22–24 AMP

This final chapter, entitled "The Signet Ring and Sonship," will explore other instances of the signet ring in the New Covenant. To start off, we will look at the seal on Jesus' tomb, harkening back to the seal that King

159

Darius's officials placed on the lions' den where Daniel was placed (see chapter 6). Next, we will look at the story of the lost son (also known as the Prodigal Son) in Luke 15. By the end of this chapter on sonship, you will learn how *you* are the signet ring of the Father. He wants to bring you back to your original relationship with Him. He wants to restore your position and full authority.

The Seal on Jesus' Tomb

In part II of *The King's Signet Ring*, you read about how King Darius's officials placed a seal on the lions' den where they placed Daniel. In a similar way, Pontius Pilate, a prefect in the Roman Empire, gave them his signet ring to secure the tomb with a special seal from the Roman king, the final governmental authority and power:

> The chief priests and the Pharisees went to Pilate. "Sir," they said, "we remember that while he was still alive that deceiver said, 'After three days I will rise again.' So give the order for the tomb to be made secure until the third day. . . ."
>
> "Take a guard," Pilate answered. "Go, make the tomb as secure as you know how."
>
> So, they went and made the tomb secure by *putting a seal* on the stone.
>
> Matthew 27:62–66, emphasis added

The reference to a seal ("they set a seal") in verse 66 (NASB1995)[1] refers to *sphragizō*, meaning "to stamp (with a signet or private mark) for security or preservation (literally or figuratively); by implication, to keep secret, to attest."[2]

The Pharisees opposed the Lord Jesus Christ with every power they had. One commentator wrote: "The seal was sign of authentication that the tomb was occupied and the power and authority of Rome stood behind the seal. Anyone found breaking the Roman seal would suffer the punishment of an unpleasant death."[3] But the Pharisees were not able to stop Jesus Christ from doing God's work. God the Father was working through Him with great signs and wonders that no one could refute or stop. Finally, they decided to crucify Him. Jesus Himself told them, however, that though they would crucify Him, He would rise on the third day. After He was crucified and buried, they remembered what He had said about His resurrection.

But God, who has the true and final authority, caused an unexpected earthquake. An angel of the Lord descended, and the stone was rolled away. The seal was broken! His Son, the Lord Jesus Christ, rose out of the tomb on the third day. The angel spoke to the women who came to the tomb early in the morning on the third day: "He is not here; he has risen" (Matthew 28:6). As a result, God the Father gave His Son, the Lord Jesus Christ, all authority on earth and in the heavens. Furthermore, He qualified Him to open every seal.

We read in Revelation that when the apostle John wept because there was no one who could break the seal and open the book, he was told that there was only one: Jesus Christ. When the Lord Jesus took the book and opened it by breaking the seal, a new song of heaven burst out:

> "You are worthy to take the scroll and to open its seals, because you were slain, and with your blood you purchased men for God from every tribe and language and people

and nation. You have made them to be a kingdom and priests to serve our God, and they will reign on the earth."

Revelation 5:9–10 NIV1984

The Lord Jesus Christ, the King of kings and the Lord of lords, therefore, has all authority and the final word. The delegated authority given by the signet ring recognizes that the ring represents accountability to God. Anyone who misuses or abuses this authority knows they are accountable.

The Return of the Lost Son

The Parable of the Prodigal Son in Luke 15 is another good example of a ring as identity but also as authority. The story begins in verses 11–16:

> "There was a man who had two sons. The younger one said to his father, 'Father, give me my share of the estate.' So he divided his property between them. Not long after that, the younger son got together all he had, set off for a distant country and there squandered his wealth in wild living. After he had spent everything, there was a severe famine in that whole country, and he began to be in need. So he went and hired himself out to a citizen of that country, who sent him to his fields to feed pigs. He longed to fill his stomach with the pods that the pigs were eating, but no one gave him anything."

In this parable, the lost son came back to his senses after realizing his father's servants had food to spare, and yet he was starving to death. He was in a difficult situation with only one course of action. He said, "I will set out and go back to my father and say to him: 'Father, I have sinned against heaven and against you. I am no longer worthy to be called your son; make me like one of your hired servants'" (vv. 18–19). It was all he could do, since he no longer had rights without the signet ring—his identification and authority. When his father saw him from afar, however, he had compassion on him—not to make him one of his workers or even to adopt him, but to restore him into his full sonship role again. The young man didn't deserve to be celebrated as a son, but the loving father overlooked his errant behavior and said to his servants, "Quick! Bring the best robe and put it on him. Put a ring on his finger and sandals on his feet" (v. 22).

Along with the signet ring, a kingly garment is given to an anointed king to rule a nation with authority. The Lord promoted Joshua, for example, to a new level of authority over the entire nation: "Take silver and gold and make a crown, and set it on the head of the high priest, Joshua son of Jozadak" (Zechariah 6:11). Joshua was in the Lord's presence; he stood before God. When we are in our place and dwell in the Lord's presence, our true identity is restored. Likewise, when the Prodigal Son returned home, his father prepared a great feast to prove to his son he was fully accepted and loved.

The desire of the enemy is to disqualify us by using our past shortcomings, like he did with the Prodigal Son and Joshua. In the case of Joshua, the Lord rebuked the accuser, affirmed Joshua's call, gave him a new, righteous covering and gave him increased authority. The Prodigal Son's father embraced him and put a new garment on him. The practical lesson is this: When the enemy accuses us, the best thing is to be a child of God—not a lawyer trying to defend ourselves. When we walk in a father-child relationship and dwell in His presence, He is our defender. To win the war of identity and walk with full authority, therefore, our right relationship with God, our true spiritual Father, is crucial.

A New Garment of Authority

First, the father gave the son a new garment. That act removed the past shame from his life and affirmed his true identity. A garment is a sign of restoration of true identity for full spiritual authority. It is the sign of true righteousness, which is the identity of those who are cleansed and forgiven. In the book of Revelation, chapter 7, we see a beautiful picture of this:

> Then one of the elders asked me, "These in white robes—who are they, and where did they come from?" . . . And he said, "These are they who have come out of the great tribulation; they have washed their robes and made them white in the blood of the Lamb."
>
> vv. 13–14

I understand the shame of not having the right garment for the right occasion. When I was a senior in Bible school, I was chosen by the school to represent the student body and invited to go to another region of Ethiopia to speak at an annual conference. We drove two days with missionaries and some national, well-known speakers and arrived at the conference site. I had never attended, let alone spoken at a large conference like this. There were thousands of people on an open field, some under temporary shelter. I was the first speaker. But there was one problem. I didn't have suitable or formal clothes to wear. I was one of three speakers for the three days—one missionary; one national, well-known and respected; and me. The others were dressed well in ties and suits. Everyone was waiting for me to change and put on formal wear for the occasion, but I didn't have any.

Can you imagine how I felt? And the voice of the enemy? I didn't know how to respond. One missionary wife called in and said, "You don't have clothing to wear for this conference, do you?" I told her that I didn't. She brought her husband's white shirt and told me to put it on. That was great, but the problem was that her husband was very tall and big, while I was small and skinny. But they gave me the courage to put on the shirt, pull it back and hold it with my left hand, then my Bible with my right hand, and preach for three days, which I did. I still remember that message, the place and how those thousand people responded. I believe the Lord didn't let them see my left hand, only my right hand, and His hand that was upon me. He covered me with a garment of His righteousness. He became my identity because of His covenant.

A Ring as a Sign of Authority

Second, the ring the prodigal was given before he left home showed his authority, his covenant relationship with his father, his power over the estate of his father and his rights and privileges to the inheritance.

That signet ring served as identification and access to his father's wealth. It was also the signet ring's authority that emboldened him to go to his father and ask for his share of the estate. Then he left his home for a distant land. After he had wasted his money and suffered great loss, he came to his senses and decided to go back to his father.

But the prodigal had used his signet ring to get his inheritance and had given up his covenant relationship with his father. He knew he would not be able to return to his father and claim his rights as an heir. He took the money without understanding the long-term impact the broken relationship would have upon him. "After he had spent everything, there was a severe famine in that whole country, and he began to be in need" (v. 14). The resource was dried up because of the broken relationship. I know the impact of this from personal experience.

My own journey is similar. I (Alemu) was born and grew up in the countryside of Ethiopia. My father was a farmer. When I started school around age twelve, my parents initially didn't approve of my going to school. When they realized my determination, however, they accepted the reality of my decision to go to school and supported me by sending supplies to my aunt with whom I was living. Everything was going well until my family found out that I had accepted the Lord as my personal Lord and Savior. When I refused to participate in our traditional worship ritual, I was forced to leave home and run away. My relationship with my parents was broken, but I couldn't participate.

Furthermore, my father made a decision that I shouldn't go back to the missionary school. I was a newborn believer, beginning to read the Bible, and I knew I had to pray. I was not ready to give up my education. I was determined to return to school even without my father's approval and support.

When I returned to school, my aunt, who had been giving me room and board, found out about the conflict between my father and me. She waited a few days to see if supplies would be sent from my parents. When she discovered the support my parents had been sending was suspended, she told me that I could no longer stay with her. I didn't have anything for some days. I went without food for three days. I would go to a river that was close to the school and kneel down to pray and drink the brown, dirty water for my lunch and dinner. All because of the broken relationship with my father. The greatest joy of my life, however, was the day my father called and asked me to tell him about the Lord Jesus, and he prayed with me to accept the Lord as his personal Savior.

Through the signet ring, the son's identity and relationship with his father were restored immediately. Now, because of the signet ring, he regained his right to the wealth of his father and the blessings he had given up. The signet ring brought him back to his original relationship, position and full authority. The father-and-son covenant relationship was restored. The signet ring was used as a seal for this purpose. The proper identification gives a person his true identity and rights.

Is there any doubt that true spiritual authority is gained by emptying ourselves to do God's will? That means dying to self and living to fulfill God's purpose. Paul was referring to this when he said, "I have been crucified with Christ and I no longer live, but Christ lives in me. The life I now live in the body, I live by faith in the Son of God, who loved me and gave himself for me" (Galatians 2:20).

God trusts individuals with true power that impacts generations only after the post-crucifixion resurrection life that Paul refers to in the above verse. A resurrection life glorifies God. What is the source of your authority? The purpose of authority is for leadership. Accepting the office and pairing the responsibility with true spiritual authority, therefore, results in effective leadership. Without effective leadership, there cannot be an effective church, ministry or business.

Remember, the most important question leaders ask is, Who gave you authority? Truly, it's not enough to have authority. To know the Source of true authority is absolutely crucial to do the work of God.

New Shoes of Authority

"But the father said to his servants, 'Quick! . . . Put . . . sandals on his feet.'"

Luke 15:22

Lastly, the father gave his son new shoes, a picture of freedom in our life and walk. Shoes in the Old Testament culture speak about the experience of life. Taking off old shoes was a picture of letting go of the past. That was one of the reasons the Lord asked both Moses and Joshua to take off their shoes. Putting on new shoes is about transition—getting ready for a new walk. It's a sign of preparation for moving into the new by leaving the past behind. The Lord told the Israelites to eat the Passover meal "with your cloak tucked into your belt, your sandals on your feet and your staff in your hand" (Exodus 12:11). It was a transition process from 430 years of slavery into freedom.

When I was in seventh grade in our small town, the government built a new hotel. Some of my classmates went and visited the newly built hotel. We had never seen a hotel, and they told us about it and encouraged us to go and visit. I was so excited about it, and I went to visit the hotel the next day. On arrival, the guard stopped me at the gate and told me that I couldn't come in. Surprised and disappointed, I asked him the reason. "You can't enter this hotel without shoes, in your bare feet." I was so disappointed, and I felt that my freedom was taken away because of my lack of shoes. I didn't have money to buy shoes to go back and visit. I left the town without visiting that hotel. After many years had gone by, however, when I was making a hotel reservation to go to Ethiopia, I discovered a five-star hotel, the Sheraton. I made a reservation for three days. On arrival, I was the only passenger on the service bus. I wept from the airport to the hotel, remembering what I was told years ago, what the Lord had done and the transition He brought into my life because of His love and mercy. Yes, I can identify with the feeling of the Prodigal Son when his father gave him new shoes.

The Lord Jesus underscored such transition by washing the feet of His disciples. It prepared the disciples for transition into leadership as apostles. Jesus showed them the power and authority He had prepared for them after they went through the transition process. It was an act of declaration of their final destiny, a qualifying step into authority.

The Prodigal Son's covenant relationship with his father was reestablished through the signet ring and enhanced by the bestowal of a new garment and new shoes. His true identity was restored, true freedom was conferred and authority was secured as a son. Now he was a free man to live for the honor of his father with his father's full delegated authority. On returning home with a broken heart and spirit, the father accepted his son unconditionally by putting the signet ring on his finger. The signet ring sealed the full restoration of their relationship, which resulted in other provisions and blessings, such as a garment and shoes and food.

Hence, covenantal relationship is the source of all spiritual and material blessings. Paul referred to this eternal truth by saying, "Praise be to the God and Father of our Lord Jesus Christ, who has blessed us in the heavenly realms with every spiritual blessing in Christ" (Ephesians 1:3). This is the reason why the Lord Jesus also told His disciples to first seek His Kingdom and His righteousness—a right relationship—which meant other things would be added to them.

Right standing, righteousness, is all about being, not doing. God is honored more when we are in right relationship with Him than by any one thing we might ever do for Him. Restoring the signet ring and becoming the Lord's signet ring in His Kingdom, therefore, requires seeking Him first and aligning ourselves, first and foremost, with our Creator. Get to know Him! He will trust us with the signet ring again. Remember the words of the prodigal's father: "But the father said to his servants, 'Quick! Bring the best robe and put it on him. Put a ring on his finger and sandals on his feet'" (Luke 15:22). Be restored to full authority, honor, ownership, power and security!

In the Parable of the Prodigal Son, the most important thing the Lord Jesus highlighted was the father-and-son relationship. The central thing to the relationship was the signet ring—as a sign of both identity and a covenant relationship. The new garments and new shoes *meant nothing without the signet ring.*

How about you? Is your signet ring secured?

You Are His Signet Ring

> *"Set me like a cylinder seal over your heart, like a signet on your arm. For love is as strong as death, passion is as unrelenting as Sheol. Its flames burst forth, it is a blazing flame."*
>
> Song of Songs 8:6 NET

God is the Creator and Sustainer of the heavens and earth. He is the King of the universe. As Creator, He is God of all creation. As King of the universe, His authority is infallible and absolute. As such, the heavens and earth declare His glory forever. Yet among all of creation, God chose human beings to carry, reflect and declare His glory on earth. For that reason, He made humans in His own image. Since humankind is created in God's image and likeness, Adam became the first signet ring of God to leave a mark on creation. Adam lost that privilege, however, because of sin.

The good news is that the original plan and purpose of God has been restored by the second Adam, the Lord Jesus Christ, the Son of God, who came as the signet ring of the Father. By paying the price for disobedience through His death and resurrection, He qualified us to become the signet ring of the Lord again. He is the only One who can make a person a new creation to receive the approval of the Father. This new creation is not only restored to a place of covenant relationship but restored to become God's signet—to reflect God's nature and walk in a new identity with all spiritual authority. The Lord made this picture so clear through the Parable of the Lost Son. When the lost son left his father's home and went away to a far country, he gave up his signet ring, his true identity and his relationship with his father. That was why, when he came back to his senses, he said, "I am no longer worthy to be called your son; make me like one of your hired servants" (Luke 15:19).

Since a signet ring was engraved with the owner's name to identify his authority, the son also lost authority and access to his father's wealth. Without the signet ring on the finger or its seal on a document, there is no proof of identity, ownership, security, authority or authenticity. That was why the father gave the signet ring to the lost son when he returned home. By giving him the signet ring, the father declared that in spite of what had happened, the lost son would now be restored to a true sonship role with a renewed identity and authority.

You Are Redeemed to Be His Signet Ring

We have seen how ancient kings used their unique signet rings to carry their emblems, identity and authority. They used it to designate authority and honor others with identification with the king or the royal family. That is what the King of kings, the Lord Jesus, did for you and me. He made us partakers of the divine nature and secured our salvation and relationship with Him by the seal of the Holy Spirit. Through that sealing of the New Covenant, He brought us into the royal family to be the King's signet ring in the world as we declare His goodness.

The apostle Peter summarized this truth beautifully. "You are a chosen people, a royal priesthood, a holy nation, God's special possession, that you may declare the praises of him who called you out of darkness into his wonderful light" (1 Peter 2:9). According to this eternal truth, each child of God is the signet ring of the King, Jesus Christ. He died as the King of Glory to bring us back to the original plan and purpose of God.

The most important concept to understand is that we are, as children of God, bought by the blood of the Lord Jesus Christ not only to receive authority to fulfill His purpose and advance His will on earth but also to become His signet ring—that is, become part of the family of God again. Although we didn't have the birthright to identify with the Almighty God as our Father, He adopted us into His family and made us partakers of His divine nature by giving us His Holy Spirit. "Because you are his sons, God sent the Spirit of his Son into our hearts, the Spirit who calls out, 'Abba, Father.' So you are no longer a slave, but God's child; and since you are his child, God has made you also an heir" (Galatians 4:6–7).

Nothing can qualify a person to be the signet ring of the King of kings except the blood of Jesus Christ. You are bought by the blood of the Lord Jesus Christ and sealed with the filling of the Holy Spirit to carry His image and declare His glory.

You Are Part of the New Covenant to Be His Signet Ring

Becoming a signet ring is not only about having the approval of God and spiritual gifts to do His work but also to carry His image and reflect His glory as we are changed into His likeness by the working of the Holy Spirit. When we carry the image of God and reflect His glory in daily activity, it is different from simply using our spiritual gifts to serve Him or others by His name. When God says to each one of His children, *You are My signet ring*, He is declaring that each person was chosen and set apart before the foundation of the earth to reflect who He is. In His great love, He preplanned for those who would accept His calling to be conformed to the likeness of His Son. The Lord Jesus gave His life to qualify us so that we can become the signet ring on the finger of God. The Lord Jesus sealed this deed by His blood and affirmed it: "This is my blood of the covenant, which is poured out for many for the forgiveness of sins" (Matthew 26:28).

The blood covenant qualifies us to be the signet ring of the King of Glory. Becoming part of God's family and carrying the image of God is the result of the New Covenant. Through this New Covenant, the Lord promised to give His children a new heart that would be faithful to God. This is an eternal, unbreakable covenant established by the blood of the Lord Jesus Christ.

You Are Loved to Be His Signet Ring

God so loved us, you and me, and gave His only Son to die on the cross to make us His children again. There is no greater love than giving one's life for another person. The beauty of the love of the Lord Jesus Christ is that He loved us when we were yet sinners, far from Him and without any hope for the future. He gave His life because of His love for us and to bring us back to an eternal relationship with God. At the Last Supper, before Jesus went to the cross, He showed the disciples the full extent of His love by washing their feet to establish their new identity as children of God. The apostle John summarized this amazing truth: "To him who loves us and has freed us from our sins by his blood, and has made us to be a kingdom and priests to serve his God and Father—to him be glory and power for ever and ever! Amen" (Revelation 1:5–6).

God our Father also poured His love upon us, the same love He has for His Son, the Lord Jesus Christ. The apostle Paul, who understood and was motivated by the love of Christ, declared that the depth, width and height of His love is beyond comprehension. To make us again the children of the King of Glory, the Lord Jesus loved us with the same love the Father has for His Son. Such love is what qualifies a person to be the signet ring of the King. If you have accepted fully His love and have given your life to Him, you are His signet ring. He carries you in His hand, and no one can snatch you from His hand or separate you from the love that is in Christ Jesus.

You Are Called to Be His Signet Ring

The Lord Jesus started His ministry by calling the Twelve to Himself. When they decided to follow Him, they came to be with Him. The significance of this calling was that He set them apart for the greatest responsibility—to carry on what He came to do. For that reason, He prayed all night before He called them to Himself. The fact that the Lord Jesus prayed all night about the call of the disciples shows the magnitude of the matter. The purpose of His calling was to authorize them for their assignment. "He appointed twelve that they might be with him and that he might send them out to preach and to have authority to drive out demons" (Mark 3:14–15).

This is the process of receiving the signet ring of approval and authority to walk with power. In this context, the call of God sets us apart so that we may carry out His eternal will as His ambassadors on earth. This is a picture of becoming His signet ring. God's call designates us to fulfill His will and purpose. The call to become the signet ring of the King doesn't start with a specific task, assignment, spiritual ministry or even Christian service. It is a call to establish and mature a *relationship*.

The call of God starts with a relationship—your relationship with God the Father, through the redemptive work of Christ, by the Holy Spirit. The call uses the two-edged sword, the eternal and Living Word of God. Indeed, the Bible refers to this relationship as the call to salvation. The desired outcome of God's call to relationship is the forgiveness of sins and eternal salvation for each one of us. Accepting this call sets us free from the outcome of sin: eternal, spiritual death. God's grace gives us the spiritual authority to become His children and bearers of the King's signet ring. Think about that: The Creator of the universe is our Father.

If we receive the call to salvation, our spiritual relationship with the living and everlasting God is well-established. With that relationship intact, we can enjoy fellowship with God and abound in the spiritual blessings of Christ Jesus. We can identify ourselves with Him and be worn on His finger like a signet ring to represent Him on earth as we advance His Kingdom. The call of God is unique. A relationship with the Lord Jesus Christ requires abiding in Christ Jesus. In the Kingdom of God, everything works in the context of relationship. Everyone God has called and fulfilled for their purpose started their journey of "possible missions" by receiving God's call to a relationship. This particular call to relationship qualifies us to preach the Gospel, drive out demons and do the work of the Kingdom as an outcome of being the King's signet ring.

The disciples who accepted this higher calling and followed Jesus had their first experience of walking in Kingdom authority when the Lord Jesus sent seventy of them out, two by two. He said, "I have given you authority to trample on snakes and scorpions and to overcome all the power of the enemy; nothing will harm you" (Luke 10:19). They returned with a report that even the demons submitted to them in the name of Jesus. At this point, the Lord showed them the most important thing about relationship. He told them that He had given them power over the enemy, but they were to "rejoice that their names are written in Heaven." In other words, rejoice that you are ambassadors of the Kingdom of God with full authority as the children of God.

The final outcome of this calling is to be sent to disciple nations and people by the full authority, approval and honor of the One who has all authority on earth and in heaven. Yes, you are the signet ring of the King of Glory, designed to bring the will of God to earth. As part of the Body of Christ, you are given divine authority to bind and loose. Always remember who you are, who our God and Creator has made you to be. You are a signet ring of the King of Glory. Let me leave you with a clear picture of what that means for you: "Truly I tell you, whatever you bind on earth will be bound in heaven, and whatever you loose on earth will be loosed in heaven" (Matthew 18:18).

God continually reminds people about their authority on earth. Scripture consistently demonstrate His rule and reign. There is no other authority on earth that is able to govern His creation. Since we, His people, are approved and authorized to carry out the Kingdom mandate, we have the command to fulfill His desires. Our responsibility is to study the requirements necessary and rule with Him. His people are in partnership with God. To better comprehend the authority we have in the Kingdom of God, it is essential that we have an understanding of the authority that is available to us. The power of God, extended through our relationship with Him and Jesus Christ, our Savior, is manifest through us by the Holy Spirit.

> *You are a living signet ring. You are a chosen people who are kings and priests with the living God. Our inheritance is the reward of receiving His crown of glory and ruling with His scepter.*

Just think about it! Our authority is something that we should study and know, as this power resides within us 24 hours a day, every day. When we join the Kingdom of God, we become His children, and each son and daughter receives His rewards. His rewards include special benefits: "Do your best to present yourself to God as one approved, a worker who does not need to be ashamed and who correctly handles the word of truth" (2 Timothy 2:15).

You are a living signet ring. You are a chosen people who are kings and priests with the living God. Our inheritance is the reward of receiving His crown of glory and ruling with His scepter.

———————— **SIGNET RING DECREES** ————————

In Jesus' name, I decree that

- *I now receive a new garment from You, Father, and I allow You to remove shame from my life. I wear this new kingly garment as a reflection of Your mercy and my new identity in You.*
- *I now receive new shoes from You and let go of my past.*
- *I now receive Your signet ring, which brings me back to my original relationship, position and full authority.*
- *I am now Your signet ring, and I wear Your crown of glory and rule with Your scepter.*

CONCLUSION

A New Ring of Authority for a New Era

CHUCK D. PIERCE

My son Daniel has always loved gems. Since he was young, he would collect key gems. He would save his allowance, and instead of buying toys, he would buy gems (or reptiles, including snakes, but that is for another book at another time). By the time he graduated from high school, then the Police Academy, and married his wife, Amber, he had quite a collection. She was as into gems as he. She had an eye for the best and most precious.

A precious gem is a naturally occurring material desirable for its beauty, valuable in its rarity and sufficiently durable to give lasting pleasure. The true worth of a gemstone can only be measured by its owner because of the pleasure that its beauty brings. Carat, clarity, color and cut are the four measuring yardsticks of a precious gem. Each one of these yardsticks can have other yardsticks to measure the quality of a gem.

In 1 Peter 2:4–5 (AMP) we find these instructions:

> Come to Him [the risen Lord] as to a living Stone which men rejected and threw away, but which is choice and precious in the sight of God. You [believers], like living stones, are being built up into a spiritual house for a holy and dedicated priesthood, to offer spiritual sacrifices [that are] acceptable and pleasing to God through Jesus Christ.

In the Introduction, I shared a dream that Amber had about restoration and inheritance, which also included rings. Just after having this dream, I asked her and Daniel to inventory jewelry and other items of value that had been donated to Glory of Zion. Among these items were many rings set in gold with diamonds and other gemstones. This led Daniel to write me and share,

> When I heard Amber's dream, I immediately saw that the person who was accompanying her, Andrea, represented her salvation and the turning point of her inheritance going from a world structure to existing in the Kingdom of heaven. She was in her grandmother's house, which portrays something that has yet to be restored on that side of her family. The Lord was revealing that she has a portion that she hasn't seen, but in reality is there.
>
> When Amber found the rings in her dream, God reminded me of the rings we had just inventoried and said very clearly, *Your inheritance exists in Me, and I hold it in My hands. It has already been inventoried and accounted for, and I have set it aside for you.*

In our lives God has used restoration to help us understand how His Kingdom operates in principles of inheritance. We have watched Him restore portions of inheritance in areas we never could have imagined. We have seen how faithful He is in the restoration of things that have been lost due to iniquity in past generations.

Amber and I have watched God restore everything in our inheritance that was key to our call, and release those portions that we needed in time to complete our faith in each season. We have come to understand inheritance as both spiritual and physical.

God holds the inheritance of countless generations in his hands, and the Kingdom of heaven itself is an inheritance for those who believe. God releases the inheritance stored up in heaven, and allows that inheritance to bring us to a place of restoration in our lives. Our eyes are opened when we come to understand this, and this allows us to see the true value of our inheritance and how God would use it in ways that complete our faith.

We have personally watched God restore physical inheritances that were lost to our family in past generations, which include land, finances, livestock and many other forms of physical wealth. We have also inherited portions of the ministry call that Dad and Mom have established that are the result of a lifetime of faithfully serving the Lord and pursuing the call that God placed over their lives.

God revealed himself to my father in 1972 through a powerful experience with the Holy Spirit and from that point on began to change the course of our family's inheritance for the future. The next week, he and Mom met at the altar during a major conference they attended during their college years.

Dad shares how God first revealed Himself to him as the God of Israel, and then began to bring revelation of how honoring Israel was key to unlocking his ultimate call of healing in the nations. Dad went on to travel and serve in the nations for several decades in his dedication to fulfill that call.

When Amber and I first began our ministry together, God had us move to Israel and established our lives and call there for the first ten years. As we watch how God operates, we begin to see how He establishes our lives and direction through the inheritance we have in His Kingdom. Although we are called and have to submit individually, I have seen firsthand how the faith of past generations becomes the foundation of wisdom, revelation, and anointing that completes our inheritance and testimony in God's Kingdom. This model for inheritance is biblical, and we can see how it manifests from generation to generation in the earth.

Our inheritance and the inheritance of our family line can be based in heaven or it can be based in the earth. If it is based in heaven, then God's work in us and our family line is limitless! If it is based in the earth, then sin and iniquity gain access to hold our inheritance captive. Things lost in iniquity are restored in faith![1]

Did you know that you have a portion specifically allotted to you from God? The word *inheritance* means "my portion" (see Psalm 16:5).[2] We have all been given a space, territory or arena in which we have been granted authority. That is our portion, and how we steward this portion is key to our success in the spirit realm. In fact, the climate of our domain reflects our relationship with the Lord. He works in space and time, dependent upon faith. Our chief desire, therefore, should be for the presence of the Holy God to occupy our inheritance. You must learn to war to see His presence in your sphere of authority. This is why we ascend, gain favor and then wear His favor as a signet ring in our sphere.

A New Kingdom Era

God has a plan of triumphant redemption for each believer amid a great war over the inheritance of our future. Oftentimes, the warfare we experience is centered around internal issues. Like the disciple Peter with all of his trials, we must get beyond ourselves so we can be sent into God's mission and the destiny He has in store for us. Peter moved from being taught to being sent with revelation of the future. In this season, we need to understand how to gain access to the *breakthrough portal* we're entering into: "A portal is an opening. You're able to go through, see things you weren't able to see in other seasons."[3] This comes through your relationship with the Son through His blood and by His Spirit, which gives you access to the Father. This is how you become a signet ring and wear that ring as your identity in the earth.

Through the Son's death, He paid for your access. He is now seated at the right hand of Father, ready to give you access to triumphant counsel. Before you were ever conceived or knit together in your mother's womb, God had a distinct plan for your life. He destined you before the foundation of the earth. He knew the timing in which you would be born and the generation in which you would have the opportunity to express His love. Within that time frame, He had a purpose for you and knew what would be necessary to accomplish that purpose on the earth. We are all born in that chosen time and season. Upon your conception, God's redemptive plan began for your life. The human life cycle, designed by God, begins at the point of conception and continues through birth, the age of accountability, our spiritual rebirth, maturing faith and death before entering eternity. The process requires wisdom and counsel for each one of us to walk victoriously. In Proverbs 4:18 we find, "But the path of the just (righteous) is like the light of dawn, that shines brighter and brighter until [it reaches its full strength and glory in] the perfect day" (AMP).

The Redeemer has already paid the price for us to walk victoriously through life. We have a redemptive path. To *redeem, redemption* and *redeemer* mean "to pay the required price to secure the release of a convicted criminal, the process therein involved, and the person making the payment" respectively.[4] Our Redeemer is the Person who made that payment and is giving us access daily to reveal our freedom. Jesus has already redeemed us, therefore, from the darkness in our path of life. Psalm 16:11 says, "You will show me the path of life; in Your presence is fullness of joy; in Your right hand there are pleasures forevermore" (AMP). We must know that we have access to His wisdom, power and glory.

A Time to Gain Access

The Church is becoming a signet ring in the earth. We are learning who we are and why we are in the earth realm. Like Esther, we have a purpose for "such a time as this." Like Joseph, amid our trials, we are gaining favor to rule. We have been positioned to reign in a confused, chaotic world. Like Ruth, we must know our field or sphere to move from gleaning to harvest.

Once we understand the times, order and purposes that God is bringing from heaven, we will see a new authority begin to arise in each of us individually and corporately. This corporateness is called the Church, the *ecclesia*. This authority will cause us to be able to overthrow the enemies that have resisted us in past seasons. God will reveal new strategies of warfare that we have not considered before. With those new strategies, we will have a new place of authority in our territories.

Our faith will overcome, and our authority will give us influence. The world will begin to see us in a whole new way. We will be vital and effervescent and affect the world, ushering in a new *era of sound*.

In Joel 2 and 3, we find these statements:

> Do not fear, O land; be glad and rejoice, for the LORD has done great things! Do not be afraid, you animals of the field, for the pastures of the wilderness have turned green; . . . the fig tree and the vine have yielded in full. So rejoice, O children of Zion, and delight in the LORD, your God.
>
> 2:21–23 AMP

> Hurry and come, all you surrounding nations, and gather yourselves there; bring down, O LORD, Your mighty ones (Your warriors). Let the nations be stirred to action and come up to the Valley of Jehoshaphat, for there I will sit to judge and punish all the surrounding nations. . . . Multitudes, multitudes in the valley of decision (judgment)! For the day of the LORD is near in the valley of decision. . . . The LORD thunders and roars from Zion.
>
> 3:11–12, 14, 16 AMP

In the foreword to Paul Wilbur's book *Roar from Zion*, I wrote,

> As we are proceeding in this new era in history, we must look and listen for the "new." This new era will be summarized

as the "era in history that the Lord roared from Heaven!" He is listening for those in the Kingdom of God that will echo this same roar from Earth. . . .

In the days ahead, "there will be divine alignments and moments of change that would produce faith explosions in the Lord's people. The Lord says, 'I have power within you that I will explode!'" . . .

In a recent gathering, I shared, "We will be in a great tension—a new era of warfare for us. It won't be like the warfare we've been in in the past. It's a tension arising which I call 'The Lion vs. the Dragon War.' That will happen this decade. . . . We must leave our maintenance mentality and walk into a conquest mentality based upon the boundaries God is assigning to each one of us. . . ."

We go from faith to faith, glory to glory, and strength to strength. A new strength is coming into our inner being. This strength will result in the "Sound of FAITH" being expressed. New vision is arising. Strength means "the battle to withstand attack."[5]

This is why we must become God's signet ring corporately, territorially and generationally. Deliverers, those wearing God's signet, will rise up. Entire groups of people will begin to be delivered from the bondage and oppression that has kept them prostrate, and they will begin to stand before the Lord with great shouts of victory.

When we ascend in worship, we gain access to the hosts of heaven. This gets us into a place of wisdom with the Father. Wisdom dismantles any demon force that is attempting to overtake us. We take this wisdom and join with the forces of the hosts of heaven and the hosts of earth. This comprises a heavenly war council. This council is necessary to war for the promise ahead. We then develop a *mind* to *triumph*. We wear

His signet ring in our sphere of authority. If you are moving in this new Kingdom era, you will see several changes:

- His fullness will be seen in your personality.
- Your soul will be restored from the last season of mistakes and trials.
- All fear and manipulation that have crowded your identity and confined you to your past will leave you.
- Your new identity will reflect His ability to overcome the mountains that stopped your progress (see Isaiah 41; Zechariah 4).
- You will gain power over the enemies that would hinder your progress (see 2 Corinthians 10:3–6).
- You will steer the course of history with your prayers and acts of faith. [6]

This is a time of much confrontation. But when the confrontation of the enemy comes from intimate communion and worship, we are assured victory. This is a time when Judah (our praise and worship) must go first. Praise must become preeminent in our lives.

We must have the freedom to experiment until we come into the sound that will bring victory into the earthly realm we are to influence. "The LORD also will *roar* from Zion . . .; the heavens and earth will shake; but the LORD will be a shelter for His people, and the strength of the children of Israel" (Joel 3:16 NKJV, emphasis added).

As I mentioned in the Introduction, Esther learned to take the signet the King extended to her. She found the signet carried a sound. His roar would be before her as she led her people into battle. He roars against His covenant enemies.

His covenant people will also begin to roar and become a fearful, holy remnant to contend with in the earthly realm. He will be a shelter and a strength to those who respond to His sound and call on Him.

Worship this season will determine how the multitudes in the valley of decision begin to decide to follow God. There is an inherited roar within you. Let the Lord draw you near and develop that roar within you so that this sound is brought forth at the appropriate time in your life this season.

A Time to See, Refine Vision and Decree Your Future

There is a moment when time makes a shift. When you submit in time to the cutting hand of the Eternal Lapidarist, you gain momentum for your future. We are in that Kingdom moment now. We have not just entered a new season, but a new era in the Kingdom of God.

> In Isaiah 32:1 (TPT), the Word of God says, "Look—a new era begins! A king will reign in righteousness, and his princes according to justice!" An era is a fixed point in time from which a series of years is reckoned. An era can also be a memorable or important date or event in the history of a thing, person or nation. An era is a system of chronological notation computed from a given date as a basis. An era is a period identified by some prominent figure or characteristic feature or stage in development.[7]

We have entered a new Kingdom era. I shared more about this in *The Passover Prophecies*:

> Without a vision a people perish. In Proverbs 29:18 this word actually means that without boundaries or pro-

phetic utterance a people go backward. This is a critical
point:

    We are moving from a church *era to a* kingdom *era.*

    In this divine shift, the Lord is transforming our mind-
set so we move outwardly from what has been built in one
season into a new movement for the next season. This will
be a new building season, but first we must unlock God's
kingdom plan and align heaven and earth.

    When the Lord revealed His Messiahship to His dis-
ciples in Matthew 16, He gave Peter a prophetic word
that would transcend the ages. In Matthew 16:18–19 (my
paraphrase), He prophesied, "I will build My church, the
gates of hell will not overpower it, and you will have authority to unlock the kingdom and forbid and permit what
goes on in earth." We must remember that this prophecy
to Peter had yet to be fully revealed in reality. *The church
was still a mystery.* Therefore, when the day of Pentecost
came and three thousand were converted, Peter must have
thought, "How will we build for the future? How will the
Lord, who has ascended, accomplish this through us?"

    The disciples did not have a full concept of the meaning
of the "church." The only concept they had of spiritual
gathering was from the synagogue. The word the Lord
was using here was *ecclesia,* which was a Roman concept
of ambassadors going in to transform a region to make it
look like Rome. Everything seemed new to the disciples.
Just a few weeks prior, they had a revelation of the Lord
being Messiah. Now they had to see how to gather and
build for the future out of a new paradigm. . . .

    This would begin a whole new era in the genesis of
the early church. Now, the *Spirit of God* would help His
leadership establish something that would be indestruc-
tible. There would be unsurpassed power in the ecclesia
to overcome the enemy of mankind, Satan. But before the

church was built, there had to be an unlocking of God's kingdom power within the triumphant people who would walk into the future. . . .

We must remember it took approximately seventy years to establish the first church era. In every era we unlock a kingdom plan so we can build the prototype for the ecclesia for the future. This new era propels us into a season of unlocking so that we can build in days ahead.[8]

You Are Being Cut to Shine

One of my favorite Scriptures is Matthew 8:5–13, where Jesus heals the servant of the centurion soldier. I believe this passage is so important for individual and corporate advancement in the Church. This is the story, of course, of a Gentile leader who was concerned about his servant who was paralyzed. He presented his case to Jesus as He came into Capernaum. Jesus was touched by His presentation and said, "Shall I come and heal him?" (v. 7).

The centurion soldier told Yeshua that it was not necessary for Him to come to his house because he could understand and perceive the authority that He walked in. When one understands authority, one sees authority. So he told the Lord that all He needed to do was speak the word, and the power would find his servant and he would be healed. Jesus replied, "Assuredly, I say to you, I have not found such great faith, not even in Israel" (Matthew 8:10 NKJV). This is probably one of the most important passages for us to understand at this time.

This is the understanding of faith and authority that is needed not only to enter the Kingdom but to see the Kingdom advance. Faith works by love. Love is demonstrated through worship. Worship is the reality of the relationship between

God, the Creator and Possessor of heaven and earth, and humankind. This is how we wear the signet ring of heaven and use that authority in the earth.

Submit to Being "Cut"

The centurion came to Jesus with a request for Him to heal his servant (see Matthew 8). Being a military man, he knew how the chain of command worked. Caesar was at the top of it, and as long as the centurion stayed in his place in the chain, whatever he said would be backed up by those over him, all the way up to Caesar himself. The centurion had faith to bark commands to his men, knowing they would obey or suffer the consequences from those over him in the chain. His authority actually came from his submission. When he saw the spiritual authority that Jesus walked in, he knew it could only be because He was submitted to His authority, God the Father, and that whatever Jesus said would be backed up by God Himself. He told Jesus,

> "For I also am a man subject to authority [of a higher rank], with soldiers subject to me; and I say to one, 'Go!' and he goes, and to another, 'Come!' and he comes, and to my slave, 'Do this!' and he does it.' When Jesus heard this, He was amazed and said to those who were following Him, 'I tell you truthfully, I have not found such great faith [as this] with anyone in Israel.'"
> Matthew 8:9–10 AMP

I like how John Dickson sees this concept of faith and authority:

> Under those in authority, we have the faith to step out in authority. Because of this, I never have to defend my

own actions. If someone takes exception to what I do, I tell them to take it up with my pastor. He has given me my boundaries and he backs me up in those boundaries. He defends me. It's his job. I am a man under authority. I don't have a lot of bosses. I can't do what everyone wants me to do. Too many cooks spoil the stew, so I make sure I have only one cook: the person in charge.

"Obey your leaders and submit to them, for they keep watch over your souls as those who will give an account. Let them do this with joy and not with grief, for this would be unprofitable for you" (Hebrews 13:17 NASB).

The Scripture says that it is to our profit if we make the task of watching over us a joyful endeavor for our leaders. It is they that have to give an account, not only for us but everyone else in the church. Everyone thinks that their area is the most important thing going on, but those that watch over us have to see what is best for the whole church. They have to have a wider perspective than just our personal area of ministry and see how each one's part fits into the whole. Let's trust them to do this so their task of oversight will be a joy, not a grief. God will then make sure we profit from it because the whole church has moved forward through the combined efforts of every-one's ministry, not just our song.[9]

The boundaries are simple. We are people under author-ity. This is what gives us the authority and faith to move in the prophetic anointing. What are *your* signet boundaries?

The key to coming out shining, brilliant and ready to be used is submission to the process of being "cut" into the beautiful gem for His signet ring. Submission is the act or fact of yielding to a superior force or to the will of greater authority to become and establish a better quality of life. Remember the story of the centurion soldier?

In Matthew 8:5–10, Jesus describes his submission as an expression of faith. The centurion expected his soldiers to submit to him because he had submitted himself to the authority of the emperor. That meant that by submitting to the centurion, the soldiers were, in fact, submitting to the emperor himself.

They didn't submit to the centurion because he was better or smarter or always right. They submitted to the centurion because he was under the emperor's authority and they knew the emperor would back him up. Jesus called the centurion's understanding of this the greatest faith He had seen in Israel. The centurion used the signet of the emperor justly, and it resulted in making his servant whole.

The Father Gives Us His Signet

Just like the centurion, we must learn to submit to authority. Knowing the Father—the One who gives us His signet and to whom we submit—is vital.

God has revealed Himself as Father, Son, and Holy Spirit. Father is the first person of the Trinity. He sent His Son into the earth to be the perfect and infinite object of His love. He is the 'Father of our Lord Jesus Christ' (1 Peter 1:3; 1 Corinthians 8:6; Ephesians 1:17). Yeshua taught His disciples to address God in prayer as "our Father." He did not use that form Himself.

He is the Father of the Jewish nation. Israel is not like other nations. Israel is 'the nation.' The chosen nation owed its origin and continued existence to His miraculous power and special care. Israel is a people and a land with the Torah. As their Father, He loved, pitied, and rebuked them. Also, He required obedience of His people. As a good Father, He disciplined them until they learned the joy of submission. *He has a fatherhood.* God is represented as the Father of various objects and orders of beings that He has created. He is 'the Father of lights,' the heavenly bodies (James 1:17). He is also 'the Father of spirits' (Hebrews 12:9). He is particularly the *Father of man.* We are created after His image (Acts 17:26; Luke 3:8).

Let the redeemed say so! He is Father of the redeemed. Those who receive Him as Father are actually saved through the Son, Jesus Christ, and admitted to the privileges of children in the divine household. This is how adoption works. . . .

Adoption simply means you receive the privileges of a natural son or daughter. We find examples in the Bible of both male and females experiencing this. Abraham even mentioned that he had adopted his slave, Eliezer, as one of his sons. In Roman culture, the adoption of a stranger into a bloodline caused that stranger to become a member of a family. This tie could not be broken. . . .

Adoption is a positional word not just a relational word. I think many people don't understand their time or place since they don't understand the position of adoption they have with their Creator or Father. Many people really never experience God's love for them.[10]

This is how we receive our signet ring. We have a Father who loves us, knows everything we have done and still wants to adopt us so He can bring us into our created purpose and destiny. My wife, Pam, and I adopted two children, so we personally know the power of adoption. Our choice not only gave them legal standing in our family and access to everything we have positionally, but it also expressed our love and desire to have relationship with them as our children. So many people feel abandoned and disconnected—not recognizing their relationship as a son or daughter of the heavenly Father also positions them to gain access to all the privileges of children in the divine household. That is truly how adoption works and how we receive access to the signet ring.

Knowing the Father

For many, our relationship (or lack of relationship) with our earthly father greatly impacts how we perceive and relate to our heavenly Father. In *Time to Defeat the Devil*, I shared the following about my earthly father:

> I loved him dearly, but I watched him stray from God, seek a life filled with lawlessness, get caught in a myriad of schemes, and end in destruction. One day when I was driving to work, however, the Lord's presence filled my car. His power was so tangible that I had to stop the car and pull to the side of the road. He poured His love into the car and into my heart. I said, *"Lord, what have I done that You would manifest Your love to me like this?"* The Lord said, *"This is how much I loved your father."*
>
> I immediately saw the love of God in a way that I have never seen His love for His children. No matter what my dad did, God's love was unchanging. My dad rejected that love, but the love was there and available. Once I saw the love of God for my earthly father, knowing how evil had penetrated and captured him, I saw God's love as pure and holy.[11]

Jesus said, "Is there anyone here who, if his son asks him for a loaf of bread, will give him a stone? . . . So if you, even though you are bad, know how to give your children gifts that are good, how much more will your Father in heaven keep giving good things to those who keep asking him!" (Matthew 7:9, 11 cjb). Knowing His love is akin to wearing His signet ring in the earth.

Worship in Spirit and Truth

In another setting, Yeshua defined the experience of worship in John 4:23–24 (AMP):

> "But a time is coming and is already here when the true worshipers will worship the Father in spirit [from the heart, the inner self] and in truth; for the Father seeks such people to be His worshipers. God is spirit [the Source of life, yet invisible to mankind], and those who worship Him must worship in spirit and truth."

This defines the reality of the relationship between God and man.

He needed to go to Samaria to mend a breach between the Samaritans and the Jews. He met a woman with a terrible reputation at Jacob's Well in Samaria. This woman dropped her pot and her past, put on His signet ring and led the whole region into His love and grace.

You Are the Gem in His Signet Ring

The process of cutting and polishing gemstones is called *lapidary*. Gemstones that have not been cut or polished are considered "rough." Lapidary techniques include sawing, grinding, sanding, lapping, polishing, drilling and tumbling.[12] That sounds pretty ominous when you think of a raw stone. As I quoted earlier, you are a precious stone that is being fitted for a great purpose. You are actually going through this process in your life. Your circumstances, the trials you are going through and the atmosphere around you are all being used as a part of your "cut." The Lord is using everything in your life to get you fashioned for His signet.

In *The Worship Warrior*, a book I co-authored with John Dickson, we discuss the great transitions that heaven and earth are going through. Even as I write this chapter, we are seeing how nations are falling and rising in ways that would have seemed impossible a few decades ago.

As God's people, we are the central theme of the transition. Transition means crossing over from one place or dimension to another. Transition is also a shift in sound or a musical modulation, or a passage leading from one section of a piece to another. Sound creates movement. Worship and sound are important. Open the window and receive the sound of the Lord! Let the wind of the Spirit bring the sound that you need through the window of heaven and into the place where you are standing.

Your conscience is like a window between soul and spirit. Make sure nothing is clouding your conscience. Sound that leads you into movement and worship will cause your conscience to remain in alignment with God. The conscience is one of the absolute authorities of our life. When our conscience is aligned and interacting with the Word of God, the 'window' remains clean and open. The conscience is the lamp of the body. The conscience is the eye of our spirit that causes us to see into the heavenly realms.

We say what we see! Open your mouth and release the decree that is in your heart! This is the season of confession and decree. What we say now determines our future. If we will cleanse our conscience, then the revelation that has not been able to influence our minds will find entrance.

Let the shout of the Lord arise in you. Let your confidence in the Lord be heard. Though the enemy is roaming like a mighty lion, seeking whom he may destroy, there is a roar in *you* to be released at this time. This roar will defy the enemy. Go past that which seems invincible in your life. Get in the river of change that is flowing by your door and let it take you to your next place. Get a shield of protection around you. Birth the *new* that the Lord has for you. Your latter end (future) will be greater than your beginning!

There is a violent sound arising in the earth. This is the sound of God's people praising! As you praise "violently," you are releasing the '*Roar of the Lord*' that has been held captive in God's people. Let me explain the '*Roar of the Lord.*' God's sound permeates from heaven and orders much of what goes on in the earthly realm. When He is ready to bring restoration to earth, He releases His sound. Judah goes first! Judah roars! The roar of God is within us.

Lord Sabaoth is just as strong in the New Testament as He is in the Old Testament. He is the Lord of the armies. There is a sound connection from heaven when His armies enter the earth and align with us, His Kingdom people. This is a season to help people find their place and operate in the diversities of their gifting and administrations in the army. Your gift is needed in the Body! Your praise is needed in the earth. You are needed for a time 'such as this' to bring heaven's changes into earth's atmosphere."[13]

Revelation 5:5 tells us that Jesus is the Lion of Judah. That Lion is living in us. Satan only roams about "like" a roaring lion. Jesus *is* a roaring lion. We have to let that aspect of praise be in us. That Lion in us is strong, confident, aggressive and not to be roused: "They will walk after the LORD, He will roar like a lion; indeed He will roar" (Hosea 11:10 NASB). There is a sound of God being released in the earth right now through His people that is signifying the strength of God in these times. The enemy is walking around like a roaring lion seeking whom he will devour, sounding accusations and producing fear. God is releasing His roar, which is much greater than the enemy's.

The Lord is saying,

Let Me bring forth a new expression of worship. Let it take you beyond where you have been with Me before. For I have increased My activity in the heavens—there is a new release of the angelic forces that are My Triumphant Reserve for just this—your time in history! Don't allow the stirring of the second heaven realm to cause you to shrink back—but instead, rush toward the Roar of Heaven that I am releasing in this hour. This is an Awakening Roar—a declaration of War Roar and a Releasing Roar that will cause keys of revelation to unlock the treasures of the ages! Treasures held for you and treasures planted in you. Remember the last chapters of My Covenant Book—you win! For "I AM" the One who has never lost a battle!

Once you taste and experience the glory of God, nothing else will satisfy you. His glory is the weightiness or heaviness of His honor, splendor, power, wealth, authority, magnificence, fame, dignity, riches and excellency resting upon us, or in our atmosphere. His glory is so real that it is tangible. His glory is the opposite of the vanity of the world. Eventually,

His glory will fill the earth. As the prophet Habakkuk said, "His glory covered the heavens, and the earth was full of His praise" (3:3 NKJV). He began his prophecy by saying, "For I will work a work in your days which you would not believe, though it were told you" (1:5 NKJV). The Lord's original purpose in our creation was for us to live in His glory. Garden life represented both work and worship engulfed by God's glory. We are on the verge of a great glory shift. This will cause God's Kingdom people to triumph and be recognized in a new way. As Yeshua says, they will perform miracles and works even beyond the things that were seen in His day.

Submit to the Eternal Lapidarist. Get ready to be brilliant and shine. Be His signet ring as you move and live in the earth. Wear the signet ring! This will accomplish seeing God's Kingdom come in its fullness; we must understand how to pray and position ourselves for the future.

> "Arise [from spiritual depression to a new life], shine [be radiant with the glory *and* brilliance of the LORD]; for your light has come, and the glory and brilliance of the LORD has risen upon you. For in fact, darkness will cover the earth and deep darkness will cover the peoples; but the LORD will rise upon you [Jerusalem] and His glory and brilliance will be seen on you."
>
> Isaiah 60:1–2 AMP

Get ready for a great shaking! Thrones of iniquity are going to fall. We are about to see a tremendous shift in worship throughout the world as God's throne is reestablished and the Church rises into a new glory. One New Man is arising! A King is coming!

NOTES

Introduction

1. "Fisherman's Ring," *Encyclopedia Britannica*, https://www.britan nica.com/topic/fishermans-ring.

2. Anne Tate, personal communication, August 22, 2021.

3. Justin Rana, personal communication, August 25, 2021.

4. Charlie Campbell, Yunnan Yuxi, and Alice Park, "Inside the Global Quest to Trace the Origins of COVID-19—and Predict Where It Will Go Next," *TIME*, July 23, 2020, https://time.com/5870481/coronavirus -origins/.

5. "Policy Responses to Covid-19," International Monetary Fund, https://www.imf.org/en/Topics/imf-and-covid19/Policy-Responses-to -COVID-19.

6. Justin Rana, personal communication, August 26, 2021.

7. Chuck D. Pierce, *One Thing: How to Keep Your Faith in a World of Chaos* (Destiny Image, 2011), 168.

8. See Isaiah 55:12.

9. See 2 Samuel 5:24.

10. Chuck D. Pierce, *Redeeming the Time: Get Your Life Back on Track with the God of Second Opportunities* (Lake Mary, Fla.: Charisma House, 2011), 207.

11. Amber Pierce, personal communication, August 26, 2021. Amber shares the full story about her family in *Joy in the War: Expand Your Ability to Embrace Hope in the Heat of Battle* (Charisma House, 2021).

Chapter 1 The History and Significance of Signet Rings

1. Nic Screws, "Everything You Need to Know About Wearing a Signet Ring," *Bloomberg*, August 24, 2015, https://www.bloomberg.com /news/articles/2015-08-24/everything-you-need-to-know-about-wearing -a-signet-ring.

2. Screws, "Everything You Need to Know."

3. See also Exodus 35:22.

4. *Rawlinson's Hist. Illus. of the O.T.*, 46, quoted in "Seal," *Easton's Bible Dictionary*, Bible Study Tools, https://www.biblestudytools.com /dictionaries/eastons-bible-dictionary/seal.html.

5. "Seal," *Easton's Bible Dictionary*, Bible Study Tools, https://www .biblestudytools.com/dictionaries/eastons-bible-dictionary/seal.html.

Chapter 3 Signet Rings as Symbols of Kingly Authority

1. Don Crum, sermon, January 27, 2021.

2. *Merriam-Webster.com Dictionary*, s.v. "dynasty," https://www.mer riam-webster.com/dictionary/dynasty.

Chapter 4 The First Biblical Mentions of the Signet Ring

1. "Seal," *Easton's Bible Dictionary*.

2. "'Signet' in the Bible," Knowing Jesus, https://bible.knowing-jesus .com/words/Signet.

3. Dikkon Eberhart, "What Christians Should Know about the Pentateuch," Bible Study Tools, Feb. 23, 2019, https://www.biblestudytools .com/bible-study/topical-studies/what-christians-should-know-about-the -pentateuch.html.

4. "Judah (2)," *International Standard Bible Encyclopedia*, Bible Study Tools, https://www.biblestudytools.com/dictionary/judah/.

5. "Judah (2)," *International Standard Bible Encyclopedia*.

6. See the Introduction of *The King's Signet Ring* for more information on Joseph.

Chapter 5 Kings, Prophets and Priests

1. M. G. Easton, *Easton's Bible Dictionary* (New York: Harper & Brothers, 1893).

2. Easton, *Easton's Bible Dictionary*.

3. "2,600 year old seal discovered in City of David," *The Jerusalem Post*, April 1, 2019 , https://www.jpost.com/Israel-News/2600-year-old -seal-discovered-in-City-of-David-585321.

4. J. W. L. Hoad, "Promise," in D. R. W. Wood, I. H. Marshall, A. R. Millard, J. I. Packer and D. J. Wiseman (Eds.), *New Bible Dictionary*

(Leicester, England; Downers Grove, Ill.: InterVarsity Press 1996, 3rd ed.), 964.

Chapter 6 A Nation Exiled and Restored

1. Lori Stanley Roeleveld, "Who Was Cyrus in the Bible, the Man Who Allowed Israel to Rebuild?," Bible Study Tools, November 15, 2021, https://www.biblestudytools.com/bible-study/topical-studies/who-was -cyrus-in-the-bible.html.

2. W. A. Elwell and B. J. Beitzel, "Cyrus the Great," *Baker Encyclopedia of the Bible*, vol. 1 (Grand Rapids: Baker, 1988), 458.

3. "Darius," *Easton's Bible Dictionary*, Bible Study Tools, https:// www.biblestudytools.com/dictionary/darius/.

4. "Who was Zerubbabel in the Bible?," Bible Study Tools, August 8, 2019, https://www.biblestudytools.com/bible-study/topical-studies /zerubbabel-in-the-bible.html.

5. Mike Nappa, "Who Was Zerubbabel in the Bible?," Christianity .com, July 24, 2019, https://www.christianity.com/wiki/people/who-was -zerubbabel-in-the-bible.html.

6. "Who was Zerubbabel in the Bible?," Bible Study Tools.

7. Matthew Henry, *Matthew Henry's Commentary on the Whole Bible: Complete and Unabridged in One Volume* (Peabody: Hendrickson, 1994), 1567.

8. Robert Jamieson, A. R. Fausset and David Brown, "Haggai 2:23," *A Commentary, Critical, Practical, and Explanatory on the Old and New Testaments* (1882), Bible Hub, https://biblehub.com/commentaries /haggai/2-23.htm.

9. "Xerxes," *International Standard Bible Encyclopedia*, Bible Study Tools, https://www.biblestudytools.com/dictionary/xerxes/.

Chapter 8 The Signet Ring and Sonship

1. Interlinear English (NASB), Blue Letter Bible, https://www.blueletter bible.org/niv/mat/27/1/t_conc_956066.

2. "G4972 – sphragizō," Strong's Definitions, Blue Letter Bible, https:// www.blueletterbible.org/lexicon/g4972/niv/mgnt/0-1/.

3. Don Stewart, "What Precautions Were Taken to Keep the Tomb of Jesus Secure?," Blue Letter Bible, https://www.blueletterbible.org/faq /don_stewart/don_stewart_247.cfm.

Conclusion

1. Daniel Pierce, personal communication, August 27, 2021.

2. Chuck D. Pierce and Rebecca Wagner Sytsema, *Possessing Your Inheritance: Take Hold of God's Destiny for Your Life* (Grand Rapids: Baker, 2011).

3. Chuck D. Pierce, "Zion 2018," Aglow International GLOBAL CONFERENCE – BOUNDLESS, January 7, 2018, https://s3.amazonaws.com/media.tfc.org/Chuck-Pierce-Zion-2018.pdf?mtime=20180116130429.

4. "Redeem, Redemption, Redeemer," *Holman Bible Dictionary*, Study Light, https://www.studylight.org/dictionaries/eng/hbd/r/redeem-redemption-redeemer.html.

5. Chuck D. Pierce, "Foreword," in Paul Wilbur, *Roar from Zion, Discovering the Power of Jesus through Ancient Jewish Traditions* (Salem Books, 2021), xii.

6. Letters from Chuck, "A 21-Day Intercessory Thrust: A Time to Gain New Access!," GZI Ministries, November 29, 2018, https://gloryofzion.org/a-21-day-intercessory-thrust-a-time-to-gain-new-access/.

7. "Chuck Pierce Prophesies: We Are Entering a New Kingdom Era," *Charisma*, https://www.charismamag.com/spirit/prophecy/43387-chuck-pierce-prophesies-we-are-entering-a-new-kingdom-era.

8. Chuck D. Pierce, *The Passover Prophecies* (Lake Mary, Fla.: Charisma House, 2020), 44–46.

9. John Dickson, personal communication, July 13, 2021.

10. Chuck D. Pierce, *Time to Defeat the Devil* (Lake Mary, Fla.: Charisma House, 2011), 216–217.

11. Pierce, *Time to Defeat the Devil*, 217–218.

12. "How Are Gems Cut and Polished?," John Miller's Gemology & Lapidary Pages, http://www.finegemcutting.com/gemologypages/howcut.html.

13. Chuck D. Pierce with John Dickson, *The Worship Warrior* (Minneapolis: Chosen, 2015), 167–169.

Charles D. "Chuck" Pierce leads an apostolic and prophetic ministry in Corinth, Texas. He is the president of Glory of Zion International, Kingdom Harvest Alliance and Global Spheres. These three ministries are housed at Global Spheres Center, which also includes Beulah Acres and the Israel Prayer Garden. He continues to gather and mobilize the worshiping Triumphant Reserve throughout the world. The ministries located at Global Spheres Center participate in regional and national gatherings to develop new Kingdom paradigms. Dr. Pierce also serves as a key bridge between Jews and Gentiles as the Lord raises up One New Man. He is known for his accurate prophetic gifting, which helps direct nations, cities, churches and individuals in understanding the times and seasons in which we live. He has written numerous bestselling books, and he has a degree in business from Texas A&M University, has done master's work in cognitive systems with the University of North Texas and has a D.Min. from the Wagner Leadership Institute. Chuck and his wife, Pam, have six children and many grandchildren.

FB: chuckdpierce
Twitter: @chuckdpierce
Instagram @chuckdpierce

Dr. Alemu Beeftu, founder and president of Gospel of Glory, has a heart for training pastors, businessmen and politicians with a goal of building national leadership infrastructures. Alemu presently works with transformational leaders of various ages in 54 countries who have the calling, gifting and character to foster sustainable societal change for the Kingdom of God.

A native of Ethiopia, Alemu earned a B.A. from Biola University and master's and doctoral degrees in curriculum design and community development from Michigan State University. More than thirty years of practice in these and related fields have made him an accomplished and sought-after leadership trainer. He also continues to provide leadership worldwide for the Body of Christ.

Alemu's most recently authored books include *Rekindle the Altar Fire*, *Optimize Your Potential*, *Go Back to Go Forward* and *Breakout for Breakthrough*. Learn more at www.goglory.org.

More from Chuck D. Pierce and Alemu Beeftu

God's altar—a place of pure and wholehearted worship where our holy God can meet us—is vital to our personal lives, our churches and our nations so that we can be strengthened for every good work. In this influential call, you are invited to find your way to rebuild the place of God's presence to have your life, prayer and worship transformed.

Rekindle the Altar Fire

Stay up to date on your favorite books and authors with our free e-newsletters. Sign up today at chosenbooks.com.

 facebook.com/chosenbooks

 @Chosen_Books

 @chosen_books